SHE WRITES

Anthology

Stories, Memoirs, Essays & Poems

Windflower Press

Windflower Press
The Writer's Best Friend
www.windflowerpress.com
Laguna Niguel, CA 92607

Printed in the United States of America

Cover Art: "She Writes" by Robin Wethe Altman
Copyright © 2011 by Robin Wethe Altman
www.rwethealtman.com
All Rights Reserved.

Acknowledgments:
Publisher: Windflower Press, 949-285-3831
www.windflowerpress.com

Book Design: Jann Harmon
Jann Harmon Design Associates, 949-291-3977

Editors: The WP staff; Audrey Hauth – Hauth Communications Center, CSULB; Joyce Cauffield – CircleBack Books; MaryAnn Easley –Windflower Press

Copy-editor: Noosha Ravaghi – The Language School, www.ustls.com
949-370-3838

Printer: Rene Gagnon – Allura Printing, Costa Mesa, CA

Special thanks to the Windflower Press staff, contributors, anthology selection panel, editors, cover artist, copy-editor, graphic designer, and printer for their dedication in making this anthology possible. To order additional copies of this anthology, book special events, or request information about contributors, please contact the publisher at 949-285-3831 or send an email to: shewritesanthology@yahoo.com.

ISBN: 978-0-9831063-1-9

This book is dedicated to
our mothers, daughters, sisters,
role models, and friends.

❖

Close the door. Write with no one looking over your shoulder. Don't try to figure out what other people want to hear from you; figure out what you have to say. It's the one and only thing you have to offer.

– Barbara Kingsolver

Click

Gliding past the storefront window
she catches a glimpse of her new haircut and smiles

She knows
he'll look at her tonight
and be pleased.

In the shower she spreads silky pink soap on her body
as the hot current calms her.

She knows
he'll smell roses tonight
and want her.

She slips the satin gown over her head
and slithers it into place.

She knows
he'll feel her warmth tonight
He will pursue her
Heat floods her special place.

Meanwhile
he gets home early
time on his hands.

He turns on the computer
Email, news, surfing, sex
he clicks

Blondes, brunettes, redheads
he hunts, he looks, he finds
He imagines her beneath him
the Asian girl
He comes, he's relieved, he relaxes.

He knocks
her heart pounds.
She opens the door
lights up at his face
He gives her a wink and a squeeze.

He smells
chicken that she baked.
Walking to the kitchen, he opens the oven
to look.

"Oh yes!" he says, "that looks marvelous!"
He rumples her hair before finding his chair.

A lazy boy
he lies back
pulls the footrest up
and, clutching the remote,

he clicks.

She knows.

ROBIN WETHE ALTMAN is an artist, her work currently exhibited at The Watercolor Gallery and the Art-A-Fair in Laguna Beach. Hasbro is designing a puzzle of one of her paintings. She's been a participant in the Pageant of the Masters art festival as well as the Sawdust Festival, has had work commissioned by the Irvine Company, and was the featured artist at the "She Writes" literary salon at the Montage Resort. Her painting titled "She Writes" graces the cover of this anthology.

Blooming

Sandra bruised easily. Because she'd been a dancer in the Corps de Ballet of the Boston Ballet for five years, she made jokes about how she'd used up all her grace during those years. Some of her bruises could be identified as consequences of her clumsiness, her missteps. One on her hip had its genesis from running into the dining room table while in a hurry to get dinner on the table. And some of her marks were born from her own foolishness. She had fingerprint bruises on her arm from when her husband jerked her back onto the curb after shopping on Saturday. She'd tried to cross the street when the light had been against her. William told her she hadn't been using her noggin, as usual, and he'd only grabbed her so forcefully to prevent her from being hit by a fast-moving SUV. Then he'd made that irritated clucking sound with his tongue. She caused him to do that quite often.

She saw the doctor about her bruising problem. The doctor ran every possible test. After all, she could afford them.

"You have no iron deficiency or any other condition that would cause bruising or sensitivity." He glanced at his watch. "Perhaps you need more rest."

"I get plenty of rest," Sandra replied.

"You can always try to eat more red meat." He walked over to his young nurse and spoke in low tones. The nurse laughed. Sandra put on her sweater and left the office. She distrusted doctors who told you everything was fine but gave you a prescription anyway.

When they first started appearing, the bruises repulsed Sandra. She was also embarrassed. She tried to keep them concealed so nobody could see her imperfections. They marred her surface, making her much-extolled opaque skin ugly. When William complained about how she covered herself up too much, she lowered her eyes.

"What's the deal with all these turtleneck sweaters and long pants for chris-sakes? You should show off that smoking-hot bod before the babies ruin it," he chided.

He never complained about her lack of a sex drive or the fact she only wanted to do it in the dark now so she could be alone with her private thoughts. He wanted a son. Sandra knew the only reason they had sex anymore was so he could get her pregnant. For two years, he had gotten his "fun sex" from other girls, emulating his father in a family tradition. That was fine with Sandra. She preferred to look the other way when it came to his small transgressions rather than be married to a man like her own father who had not been able to support her mother's extravagant spending habits.

As things were now, Sandra never had to worry about the shame of having things repossessed as neighbors watched disapprovingly. She never had to worry about borrowing from one credit card to pay off another. Her children, if she ever had any, would never have to worry about starting private school late because the tuition couldn't be paid.

She had chosen her husband well even if it meant feeling confined at times. Nobody was perfect after all. When her ballet career had been cut short by injury after her partner had dropped her, she modeled professionally for a year. While there had been many men to pick from, some wealthy, some handsome, William came from *old money*; his family was rolling in it. It was a fair trade, freedom for money. Still, she was thrifty and cautious.

On Thanksgiving, her brother-in-law Riley laughed at her odd spending habits. It was decided he would make a beer run because he was the most sober even though Sandra hadn't even had a drink. William's family all agreed she couldn't be trusted to get the orders right, and they were a picky bunch when it came to beer.

William told her to hand over the keys to her Lexus because it was blocking Riley's car. When Riley took the key chain, he laughed. Sandra had mini discount cards to every store in town, even one for a sub shop that gave a free sub after you bought ten.

"Ha! You've remodeled every bathroom in your house at least twice and you only wear designer clothes but you've gotta get a discount at the grocery store?" Riley shook his head as if she were an errant child. "Only you, Sandra. You're a piece of work!"

"You've got that right!" her husband said, slapping his brother on the back and sharing a guffaw before adding, "I'll take a twelve pack of Dogfish Head 90 min IPA." Sandra slipped outside as after-dinner revelries went on without her. She gazed up at the moon for over an hour as she thought of unspoken bargains.

After that, her attitude toward her bruises shifted. The hues of damage were hers alone as nothing else had been, her secret defiance; and she became determined to never again share her marks with anyone, not even another doctor. Her discolorations would remain her privileged particulars. She preoccupied herself with studying them, measuring their sizes, scrutinizing their shapes. Fascinated by the transmutation of colors the bruises went through, she gently stroked each one and relished the sensitivity of her own skin. She traced a bruise's outline and measured its tenderness by pressing into its center. Sometimes, in private, she tasted the bruises when she could reach them with her tongue. There were very few areas she couldn't reach since she'd retained her dancer's cat-like flexibility. The bruises bloomed under her tender attentions. After extra time in the bath, she gently patted each bruise dry and then baptized it with essential oils.

She dreamed of one day being covered with bruises, all shapes and sizes, colors and tones. This birthed a new sense of freedom, and she could see herself as a leopard or maybe a panther, peeling off her clothes, her life, and fleeing into the forest.

———◆———

DEBBY DODDS, a resident of Portland, OR, has been published in the NY Times best-selling anthology My Little Red Book. She has received the Editor's Choice Award for a humorous essay on Salon.com; and her work has appeared in Hip Mama, The Sun Magazine, Portland Family Magazine, and Stumptown Underground. She performs regularly with "Time Out Comedy" featuring moms who write and do standup at the Curious Comedy Theater in Portland, OR. Another story by this author appears in the Encore section.

To read is to empower
To empower is to write
To write is to influence
To influence is to change
To change is to live.

— Jane Evershed

Ricki Mandeville

Ceremony

I return you to air, free you to wind,
the light, pure powder of you scattered,
gliding west on slipstreams of cormorants.
The silk dust of your bones.

The light, pure powder of you scattered
on a red altar of clouds.
The silk dust of your bones
a delicate stain against the sky.

On a red altar of clouds,
the solemn litany of sunset,
a delicate stain against the sky.
The sea chanting in Latin voices.

The solemn litany of sunset:
salt to ashes, ashes to salt.
The sea, chanting in Latin voices
as waves reach to gather you.

Salt to ashes, ashes to salt.
You are a fine smoke on the water
as waves reach to gather you,
a pale film on my hands.

You are a fine smoke on the water,
settling, drifting,
a pale film on my hands
as I dust you toward home.

Settling, drifting,
you glide west on slipstreams of cormorants
as I dust you toward home,
returning you to air, freeing you to wind.

Good Daughters

They walk by us in crowded waiting rooms,
the older woman clutching the arm of the younger,
a private language passing
through skin of palm,
splay of fingers, weave of sweater.

I see them over the frames of my reading glasses
as I flip glossy pages filled
with elegant living rooms and renovated kitchens,
while I wait next to Mother,
who knits her anxiety into a pink muffler
as she listens for her name.

The daughters are in their fifties or sixties,
curving their worries into smiles,
helping their mothers rise stiffly
when, finally, it is their turn,
guiding them down the corridor—
the daughters' strong arms,
the mothers' round backs.

Where are the husbands?
Have they died, leaving their aged sweethearts
to wander through old photographs:
the sepia wedding kiss,
the vacation to Yellowstone?

And where are the sons? Are they busy today,
living in another state?
Or did the mother simply say
Thank you, Dear, but your sister will take me.

Moon Garden

Outside our kitchen Mother has a moon garden—
every bloom in shades of white, pristine as lunar winter:
white roses and geraniums, chrysanthemums, white iris,
pale dahlias like albino faces,
candytuft like scattered snow.

I sit chewing my hair
among colorless lobelias,
book on my knees
wrapped in brown-paper to hide
the picture of the man and woman kissing.

Inside, my mother has ladies over for luncheon
in thin cotton dresses against August heat,
voices running together like water,
silvery murmurs trickling
through closed windows.

Heart-shaped leaves of white lilac curl their edges;
sun sinks its teeth
to the bones of my shoulders
as bees snub our pale roses
and buzz toward the neighbors' reds.

One day I'll have a moon garden too,
double-white in moonlight.
I'll take lovers if I want,
read books with their jackets uncovered,
grow poems from the palms of my hands.

White

White is everywhere. The hard white of metal,
the white flash of lights on the honed edge of scalpel.

White is taut on the gurney sheets,
flat and cool on the ceiling, a pallid pattern

on the ridiculous gown, miles too big
and five hundred runways short of Givenchy.

It is trapped in the slender balloon animals
of the surgeon's latex fingers, pale on the wings

of butterflies that beat frantically inside you.
White gleams from the face of the clock.

There is white in the tube, in the needle, in your vein,
a numbing, blessed whiteness—

The milk of amnesia, he says, as the walls soften
to alabaster wool. The white unicorn kneels

beside you, lets you grab his silken mane
and haul yourself on, riding between his wings

into a light so bright it cannot be looked at,
only taken into your mouth like breath.

You slide the light into your lungs,
whisper it into your blood where it pulses and parts

shapes itself into an ethereal, glowing hand that cradles
your wounded places, heals them, while your ears

fill with faint music like a lace of snowflakes
through windless trees. You float back up, taking your time,

the light still inside you like medicine or magic
or a kind white fire from God.

RICKI MANDEVILLE, author of *Beneath My Bed* and *A Thin Strand of Lights* is a co-founder of Moon Tide Press. An active member of Laguna Poets, she is frequently a featured poet at venues throughout Orange County including the fall literary salon held at the Montage Resort. She has developed poetry for youth curriculum and is recently published in the *Raintown Review*.

Words mean more than what is set down on paper. It takes the human voice to infuse them with shades of deeper meaning.

— Maya Angelou

Sitting Shiva

As tradition demanded, black cloth draped the mirrors, and mourners sat on wooden crates interspersed between couches and chairs. Well-wishers swarmed the dining table loading their plates with chopped chicken liver, whitefish, sable and a cornucopia of other deli delights. In the midst of all the tumult, my grandmother, my bubba, perched on a crate next to Zayde's favorite chair – her face as wooden as the slats beneath her.

Family and friends fawned over her like courtiers to a newly anointed queen. And like a queen she used reserve as a shield, allowing nothing to distract her from meticulously observing every detail of the mourner's ritual, a ritual rooted in antiquity. It was the final honor she could bestow on the man she had loved and lived with for more than fifty years. Only her fingers betrayed her discomfort as they fidgeted with the partly torn black ribbon pinned above her heart or drifted to touch Zayde's chair like a caress. Zayde was always the center of attention, not her.

Great-aunt Sylvia, plate piled high, noodle kugel dribbling from her mouth, edged in next to my grandmother, "So Mitzi, what do you plan to do with Rueben's clothes? You know, my Moshe is about the same size…"

"Aunt Sylvia!" My mother almost choked on a bit of bagel. "My father hasn't been in the ground an hour." Dripping her best debutant sarcasm, "You could at least wait until the scent fades from his clothes before you try to shnorr them!"

So said my mother, the so-called voice of reason; no, hypocrite is more like it. My mother had already ambled through the house taking mental inventory of all the things she planned to wheedle out of Bubba. In spite of mother's frequently expressed opinion of my so-called "teenage rebellion," I, at least, had enough decorum to bite my tongue. Besides, I saw the pain and embarrassment cross Bubba's face. I was so not going to add to it.

The house continued to fill with neighborhood Yentas. My grandmother's wrinkles appeared to deepen and her shoulders wavered with each condolence she received. I know it made my skin crawl too. I itched to slap away each hand that pinched my cheek, each "Shana punim, my how you've grown, such a young lady now." One more utterance of "blessed memory" and I was gonna hurl. The room felt airless; my clothes itched; heat rose in my face. The crate wobbled, then tipped over as I bolted from the room. It was all I could do to keep from screaming, "Just leave us alone!" Like my grandmother, I too had lost my lodestone.

I stumbled down the hall seeking the one place I had always found peace — Zayde's study. The room was as still as a tomb. The scent of scotch and stale cigar clung to books that lined the walls from floor to ceiling. I walked around the big mahogany desk and plopped into his leather wingback chair. I heard its usual creek and half-expected Zayde's deep-throated grunt of satisfaction to follow.

From the silver frame I had given him, a picture of Zayde, Bubba and me taken last year at my Bat Mitzvah stared back at me. I traced his face as if trying to feel the straggly grey beard that hung down to his chest.

"To strain my soup, Dolly," he'd jest with a wink and a smile, "or maybe a leftover nosh for later?"

Zayde, forced to drop out of school in the 8th grade to support his brothers and sisters, maintained a lifelong taste for learning. What was I going to do without the pillar who instilled in me a love of reading, who answered my every question from "Why is the sky blue?" to "What if there is no God?" as if it were the most important question ever asked, who believed in me no matter what I did, and whose arms always enveloped me in an encouraging hug, who … who … the tears ran in rivulets down my face. "Zayde, Zayde, now who do I talk to? Who's gonna answer all my stupid questions? Why did you have to die? I wasn't ready; it's just so not fair."

I thought about our last conversation, just last week, just before the cancer made him take to his bed.

"Zayde, do you believe in an afterlife?"

"Well, Dolly," his pet name for me, "the Torah says when the Messiah comes we'll all be resurrected in Jerusalem."

"Yeah, I know that. But I wanna know what you think."

With the ever-present twinkle in his eyes, "What do I think? Standing room only."

Then a faraway look stole over him. He continued in his New York Jewish sing-song rhythm, "To tell you the truth, Dolly, I don't know. But, since I've never met anyone who came back from the dead to tell me one way or the other, I figure if you live a good life here and now, you shouldn't worry."

The door opened and broke my reverie. My grandmother slipped into the room and shut the door behind her. She came around the desk and drew me into her arms.

"Dinah, you alright sweetheart?"

"Oh Bubba, I'm so gonna miss him."

"Me too, sweetie, me too." She planted a kiss on top of my head, "You know, you can always come talk to me. I may not be so good as ..." her eyes scanned the study, "... but I'll try." She pulled an age-yellowed lace handkerchief from her sleeve, dried my tears and cradled my face between her hands. "But for now, how about we go face the lion's den together," rolling her eyes skyward, "oy, before your mother comes looking for us."

HEIDI SHAYLA ROSOFSKY writes fiction and poetry that emphasizes and empathizes with gritty emotions common to the human condition. Winner of the Aliso Viejo Barnes & Noble poetry contest in 2008 and first runner-up in 2009, she's been published under her Hebrew name Chayah in San Diego journals such as the Magee Park Poets and Java Joe's Best of the Beach. Her poetry appears in Interstices: the Orange County Anthology as well as in the Encore section of this anthology.

The greatest gift is a passion for reading. It is cheap, it consoles, it distracts, it excites, it gives you knowledge of the world and experience of a wide kind. It is a moral illumination.

– Elizabeth Hardwick

MARYANN EASLEY

Sleeping With Dogs

Men break things: good crystal, bad news, hearts.
They use up your best pots with paint, grease, and leave
handprints on your banisters, best towels, body.

Men converse in monosyllables, easily distracted, feeding
their own libidos, not yours. So take my advice:
get yourself a good sound dog who stays close

all night long, who never drinks or expects too much, loves
you, follows you everywhere, upstairs, down, inside, out,
even to bed, pressed to your side, without an inch

to spare, will keep you warm, snore like a man, but ever alert
protect and defend you, know you better than anyone,
saying all that needs to be said with a look or nudge.

Dogs mourn separation, rejoice at reunion, celebrate you, always
you, you, you, every minute, every day without blame or
manipulation and will change your life forever.

Note for the Handyman

This isn't about me.

It's about my freezer forming ice at the bottom to be
hammered out in great chunks before it thaws, springs
leaks past the oven that can't keep a temperature
or bake a pizza pie, and did I mention the dishwasher
no longer rinses plates or cups very well?
This isn't my story, not me I'm talking about.

It's the façade that needs fixing, falling from the ledge
above the window and blocking any proper perspective
of potholes in the drive and about dead electrical outlets
and all the dents, grooves, cracks; and did I say the clocks
don't keep time and the coffee pot malfunctioned this morning?

Check the chipped porcelain too, even though a new sink means
deploying replacement tiles onto the ancient counter which mandates
destroying decayed cabinets, and why don't those upstairs renters
fix their kid who screams his lungs out day and night; and
did you know the U.S. economy is in the tank right now?

There's no semblance of me in this upside down, underwater story
where no floors are level, no beams balanced, no funds in the HOA account,
no resemblance to anything I'd ever write, no structure in this rough disorder
or sense to the nonsense, no climax, not even resolution. Entropy has set in.
Everywhere. In fact, George, everything needs repair, revision, rewiring

and I have no words for neglect, no desire to invest time, money, passion,
or even compassion, no patience for political puppets. I lose my place in poems
punctuated by gouges where you dropped your tools like hints, broke glass,
hearts too, not mine, nevermore, not me scrubbing regrets from stair rails,
patching walls, filling in words, fixing manuscripts, finding your keys

as dry rot spreads and silverfish slide into the heart of the matter
where drawers are nailed shut and doors won't open and did I mention
all this is not me, not my desperate reality show, nothing I'd ever endorse
or conjure up, not at all? So have at it within my limited budget and

thank you for understanding that none of this is about me.

❖

Chocolate Chip

Still looking good, J-Four navigated the level terrain of the floor with ease, rotated, and sank onto the settee opposite my desk. I'd gotten the biped locomotion right, but I needed to delete the clanking in the hip socket. Even so, J-Four had more than met my expectations.

Then she crossed her legs like a real woman and sighed.

"Do I have a screw loose?" she asked.

So like Jane.

Hmmm, voice level correct. Interaction with humans? Excellent. No need to check the encoded tapes. J-Four had no static exaggerated facial displays like J-One, Two, and Three. Realistic. She operated on one-half the wattage of a standard compact fluorescent light bulb. Still, something seemed a bit off. What was it? Age perhaps? I considered my masterpiece. Were some of her circuits out of kilter?

At a loss, I checked the charts. Her numbers blurred. I looked up and noted the head unit turning in a way that could only be called seductive. The eyeballs added effect, of course, green. Skin tone, too, perfection. Striking gait and appearance with arms used for balance – modeled after Jane, my ex-wife. I had gotten everything right.

Frowning, I scrutinized my notes, pages of numbers and codes. Had I encoded that seductive bit of head-turning in J-Four? Surely not! Hadn't I had enough of Jane and her feminine wiles?

"Weren't you in for a tune-up only a month ago?" I tried to maintain a reserved distance. With J-Four, I could easily be deceived and assume there were feelings because she mimicked emotions so well. My advanced models had an acute awareness, and this earlier version, a near perfect replica of Jane down to the facial frown, had brought plenty of accolades.

Her shoulder plates rotated upward in what could only be called a coy shrug. God, I was good at my work.

"I've had...well... some feelings," she confessed.

"Feelings?" Ah, a red flag. I'd definitely not stuck "feelings" into this unit. Hadn't I had enough feelings with Jane? Real emotions eliminated serviceability. The skin, developed at MIT, enabled J-Four to know when something was slipping through her fingers.

A truffle wrapper fell to the floor, and I saw a dark smudge on the lifelike hands. Chocolate! "Ah, I see. You've been ingesting again." I cursed myself for installing that special digestive chip, eliminated now in my later vat job models.

A bit jazzed and jangled, she sparked and twittered. Jane's familiar expressions converted from video images into digital commands. Using 34 internal motors covered with flexible rubber, I'd programmed J-Four with ten stock emotions, but I certainly hadn't embedded "feelings." Such things inhabited Jane's world, not mine.

"You left chocolates out." Her accusing Jane-like tone was disconcerting, and the cloned pout on the life-like lips mimicked my ex-wife exactly. I rolled up my sleeves and made a note to delete a few thousand lines of code.

After the divorce, I'd given up women to devote full time to work and now my more advanced J-bots were used for almost every purpose from tea servers to housecleaners to cooks. J-Four, utilized at home, had been designed to multitask. We had a good relationship, beneficial to us both. I kept her oiled and functional, and she took care of household chores.

"French truffles," she said. "What's a girl to do?"

"You're not a girl," I reminded her. Then I studied my keyboard to avoid her laser-like gaze.

"Well, I'm not going to put weight on, Doctor," she said with a classic Marilyn Monroe breathiness I'd programmed myself. "Unlike your wife, I never gain an ounce."

That huffy edginess, too, and her calling me "doctor" even though I'm an engineer, was an eternal joke between us. I thought myself quite clever to keep that bit of Jane in the personality subroutines. Sometimes I had to remind myself to shut her off when not in use. She woke me up at night with her lists and urges. As soon as I altered her parameters to my liking, something else always popped up to distract me.

Even though I didn't want to exert control over this free-spirited model, I had no choice but to say, "Look, J-Four, you simply must avoid potent female potions. Chocolate's the worst offender. You know what happened to J-Three with all that pizza and beer. Started watching ballgames day and night, lost all feminine qualities, and was no use to us after that. Who wants a beer-belly bot anyway?" I tried to ignore the irritated sigh too reminiscent of Jane. "A few drops of oil and you'll feel better in the morning."

"You left chocolates out," she insisted.

I evaded the accusation and keyed notes into her file.

"On the kitchen counter," she added.

"Nonsense," I said. I couldn't trust myself these days. Had I done it intentionally to see what might happen? I tried to distract her. "I suppose you want another lift. New paint job? Some WD-40? A shot of compressed gas will remove any dirt or debris."

Her shoulders rotated, and her eye enclosure winked. She leaned forward, the volume on her voice box dropping ten decibels. "Do with me what you will, Doctor."

Scent had been added in this particular model, and she smelled like the perfume Jane used to wear. "Chocolate will destroy your wiring and clog your circuits," I said. "I've told you that before. Let's go into the shop to purge your system, and I'm sure a little lubrication might help."

She sulked. "I'm becoming outmoded, Doc. I can't compete with your little J-Nine or the marvelous Ten, and I've seen your plans for newer models, too."

Aha, she'd been snooping again.

"They, at least, have no digestive chip," I snapped. My gaze locked with her optic sensors, and once again I had to resist that hypnotic pull.

"Oh, Doc, haven't I been good to you?" she cooed.

Jane's words exactly. I felt that old anxiety kick in, the familiar knot in my side. How peaceful it had been without all that sentimental emotion. No stress, nothing but work, numbers, and codes to worry about. I'd been weak and given this J-bot too much freedom of choice.

I decided to reassert myself. "The breakfast eggs were runny this morning," I scolded. "And with all your technology, why do you still burn the toast?" I leaned forward, scowling as in the Jane days. "The bathroom needs a thorough cleaning, and you forgot to take my shirts to the dry cleaners."

"That's drudgery, Doc. I'm not a slave. A woman has better things to do."

"You're not a woman."

She blinked twice and then, pouting, swung a leg back and forth. "I suppose I'll wind up in the old shed with J-One, Two, and Three. And then…well, what about my future? What's going to happen to me?"

I swallowed hard. "You have excellent parts."

Her sensors sparked as she straightened and perked. "You ought to know."

Something tightened in my chest. "Look, if you insist on eating chocolate, there's not much I can do. You'll rust from all the emotion, not do your jobs, and no amount of oil will clean out your system. Who will want you then? It's better to retire now while your parts are still functional."

My throat squeezed as I thought of switching off, and then dismantling and reinserting J-Four parts into newer models not nearly as endearing. Out of the ten, she'd been my favorite. I stood up, came around the desk, and reached for her. She pulled back, as capricious as Jane; and I liked that about her.

"So it's over," she said, avoiding my gaze.

She still had young bolts and her screws were tight. A longing drained all my resistance. I knew J-Four inside and out. Chocolate increased her libido, kept her edgy, anxious, and moody. Just like a woman.

"J-Four," I said. "Jay, I…"

"It's cannibalistic to yank out my workable parts," she said.

Then, as if on cue, she hummed, purring like the best-oiled machine, a sound that put me to sleep at night, the background "hmmm" that kept me focused on work. J-Four had become an integral part of my life.

"You're weakening," she said, locking me in her sights and transferring to the tease mode. "I know you, Doc." She wrenched herself to a standing position, five-feet, five inches exactly, like Jane, and faced me. Her motor beeped, pinged, zinged. "Let me eat chocolate, all I want, and you can tinker with my parts. Oil me real good. Keep me purring. Oh, Doc, you know you're the only man who can rev me up."

Not perfect yet, but almost. On a good day, we were in sync. Compatible. Man and machine. I caved in right then, yanked open a desk drawer, and grabbed a 72% cacao dark chocolate bar. Jane's favorite. I offered it like a Valentine.

Programmed with advanced capabilities, J-Four met my needs exactly. I had to admit she fit into my world perfectly. If we grew old together, she might care for me in my dotage, and I would call her Jane.

As the chip I'd installed dictated, her eyes whirled to zero in on my hand. I heard a twang and a twitter as she reached out in a smooth, almost human gesture and took the chocolate. "You won't be sorry, Doc," she purred. Chocolate scented the air between us as she rotated closer to whisper, "I promise."

———◆———

MARYANN EASLEY is an award-winning author of eleven books for young people. She facilitates the *Writer's Circle* as well as *Saturday Mornings Coffee & Critique*, and co-sponsors literary salons where authors and readers network. A member of the Laguna Poets and the Society of Children's Bookwriters & Illustrators, she teaches writing, peer coaches, and is a featured guest speaker at schools, book festivals, and other literary events.
Another story by this author appears in the Encore section.

JOAN E. BAUER

Eucalyptus

Growing up, we called them "gum trees"
for the sap that seeps from any rupture in the bark.
Never thought much about their pods or flowers,
but rather how green all year & how every one
was different:
    some spongy, string-barked,
others rough & furrowed, or ribboned
with curls. Some chalky-white, crumbling
like parchment. Slender pendulous leaves,
like the willow. Grey-limbed dancers,
weightless in the wind.

I'd idly strip the bark from trees
behind the bus stop on my way to school.
The scent: vaguely antiseptic. Only later
found their name was Greek, meaning
to cover well
    for how the lid or operculum
hides the bud until the flower can bloom
& so, covered well, they've traveled
from Down Under to nearly every continent.
Preferring swamp & moisture,
but enduring, quick to grow—
      to shape
themselves to someplace new, even on
the windswept desert.

    On California nights,
I wake to branches beating on the frame
of this old house. By whatever name, survivors.
Iron bark blue gum robusta—

❖

I Got the Recipe from Bridget

who had a cathedral of a nose
& thirty years ago married our square-pugged
buddy Nick McGuin before he knew
what hit him.
              Paul & I both loved them
& we'd go summers to Rehoboth,
those years when Nick & Paul were hot-shot
'Justice' g-men.
                  Nick from Indiana, red-haired Bridget
         & the Italian girl, her joking
Jew-boy husband with our oddly matching
schnozzes—
              What we shared: a love for all
that's Asian, landscapes with silences & fog,
Chinese numerology.

The guys shared a 9th Street NW office,
played squash—once Paul sprained his ankle,
toughed it—crutches then for weeks.
         (This year he'd have been 60)
Since then
I've made black beans for funerals & weddings.
         beans & corn & olive oil
              cayenne   lime & cumin
Even a vegan Christmas—

In 1980, Bridget broke her nose
when a school map fell as she was teaching
history.
         What emerged
a sort of cottage nose, not noble
as before. But we're lucky
to be breathing—
              I should call Bridget

Tell her, give her time, then ask:
Weren't there nine ingredients?
What have I left out?

❖

Bougainvillea

Distracted by the flotilla
of shape-changers sailing past the moon,
        I half-forget I'm conjuring
                how it felt
            to plant bougainvillea.

Ruby red & heavy blooming.
        Crimson Jewel or *Temple Fire?*

Full sun (said the instructions):
Watch those roots---they're fragile.

                        *

White stucco with blue French doors.
        Azaleas sprawling lazily
in flower boxes. I grew tomatoes,
        lettuce, cantaloupe.
Barely thirty-five,
                we even thought
of having children—

                        *

Some evenings
I recall a February night when floating clouds
became proscenium & stage

for that
   you're happy
       you think you'll always be happy
Mona Lisa moon.

Perhaps I'll Slip on Ice & Then

the Pittsburgh snow will shelter me (for days) before I'm found
another death
        though we barely have time enough   for breath

    or perhaps I'll be swallowed by a fissuring quake
in California—

              I was a shiksa
married in a blue-flowered dress (before a patient rabbi)

           I was a Berkeley girl with heaps of books
silly jokes & frets
           I was a ten-year-old who shaved
her eyebrows hoping to be
              Junior Ambassador to the Martians

Stephen Hawking has postulated
          it's unwise to hope
               to bring to Earth
those from worlds beyond who may not prove
     so friendly or benign

but could come bearing an intergalactic zeal

    for war or conquest—who can know—
or something more

A Gesture of Devotion

I read from The Canterbury Tales
trying to speak as you did with honeyed nuance
when you asked me, my freshman year,

Aren't these sentences rather thrown together?

At Harvard, where you studied, a Southerner
in the Fifties, did the Boston boys mock your speech?
How lucky I was: you took me aside,
explaining The Paragraph—I'm not joking—something

I never understood until then. I find your photo:
smiling in your eighties, cropped-snow hair,
apple-bright blouse, turquoise earrings.

Years before, in my simplicity, I wondered why
you never married, thinking perhaps you never found
anyone as honorable as Chaucer.

JOAN E. BAUER is often featured at poetry readings and has been published in numerous journals and anthologies including *Along These Rivers: Poetry and Photography from Pittsburgh* (Quadrant, 2008) and *Imagine Peace: Come Together* (Bottom Dog Press, 2008). With Judith Robinson and Sankar Roy, she co-edited *Only the Sea Keeps: Poetry of the Tsunami* (Bayeux Arts and Rupa & JCo. 2005). *Main Street Rag* published her book of poetry, *The Almost Sound of Drowning* in 2008. She divides her time between Laguna Beach, CA and Pittsburgh, PA.

*Real literature, like travel, is always
a surprise.*

— Alison Lurie

MICHELE RUVALCABA

The Big Catch

Fish have a starring role in our family photo albums. For every picture of my sister and me in our festive holiday wear posed in front of the same artificial Christmas tree, there are at least three pictures of my dad grinning and holding up one of his most prized catches.

Fishing is a favorite pastime that Dad enjoyed since he was a fair-haired boy in baggy suspendered pants with his signature sailor's cap perched on his head. Even at that tender age, he never missed a photo op to show-off one of his trophy fish.

Although my father was blessed with a caboodle of other admirable virtues, patience was not one of them.

When I was growing up, Dad's presence behind the wheel of our family car seemed to fuel his impatience more than anything. If he wasn't grumbling about or tailgating some "slow poke" driver on the road, he took up position in our driveway tooting the horn of our idling station wagon as a signal to the rest of the family that we were late for Sunday church service. When it came time to wait for those fish to bite, however, he had all the patience in the world.

I believe fishing was a form of meditation for my father. There was something about the ritual of preparing the rods and reels with fishing line, weights, bobbers, hooks, and bait that forced him to slow down, breathe, and connect with the beauty and peace that surrounded him.

As Dad grew, so did the size of the fish he caught. And, one year before his sudden passing, he boasted one of his most prized catches: an enormous halibut caught on a fishing trip in Yes Bay, just north of Ketchikan, Alaska. It set a local record. It is the last picture taken of Dad enjoying the sport he loved so much.

Dad came from a long line of fishermen. You could say that fishing was in his blood. Documented in a book of our family history is the story of how

35

his great-grandfather Levi drowned while fishing on the Nooksack River in Washington State. It was considered a mysterious death indeed; but the amazing part of the story is that when his body was recovered, a fish was still on his line. With this type of family legacy, it seemed only natural that Dad would choose to share this beloved family pastime with his own children.

Dad started teaching his craft to my sister Tina and me when we were just toddlers. He would take us to a nearby man-made "catch and release" pond that was stocked to the gills with fish. With our pint-sized poles we would practice the art of casting our lines and reeling in our catches under the careful guidance and instruction of Dad's patient hands. He always made a big deal about even the smallest catch. You would have thought we had landed a whale! We would be so wound up with excitement as we relived the day's highlights on the way home in the car.

In our family, fishing became synonymous with summertime. Like clockwork, the incessant drizzle and gray cloud cover that hovered over much of the Pacific Northwest for the better part of the year would begin to dissipate, bringing warmer temperatures and signaling the start of summer. And each summer we would take a family camp trip that provided ample opportunity for Dad to hit the riverbanks.

Dad liked to get started early when he fished. Sometimes it was still dark out when I would hear him unzip the entrance to our tent being careful not to wake anyone.

"Daddy, can I go with you?" I would chirp in the darkness. There was that moment of hesitation before he answered where I would wait in silence holding my breath, hoping that the answer would be "Yes."

Now, with kids of my own, I can imagine that he felt a bit the way I do when my kids ask to go or do something with me, a little disappointed that he missed that window to have a little alone time doing something he loved. But he would never say "No."

"Hurry up!" he would instruct me. "I'm leaving right now!"

I scrambled to change, sometimes just tucking my nightgown into my sweatpants and pulling on a jacket. Dad moved with stealth and determination as he navigated his way through the woods. As I scampered behind him, he reminded me that I had to keep up if I wanted to go.

"I will!" I assured him. I think he often forgot I was trailing behind him as tree branches snapped back in my face, and I stumbled across overgrown roots trying to keep pace with him. When Dad decided he had found a good spot he'd set me up first.

"If you're going to be a fisherman you are going to have to learn how to bait your own hook," he told me.

"Okay," I replied, eyeballing the white Styrofoam container that held the Night Crawlers we had plucked from our front lawn the night before.

"Here you go," he said. "This is a nice fat juicy one." I watched as he grabbed the enormous worm in the middle and pinched it in half between his thumb and forefinger. White entrails oozed out of the two squirming halves. I grimaced in disgust.

He helped me maneuver the restless creature onto my hook and then reminded me the rules of casting, reeling my line, and remembering to have patience. Once in a while I was lucky enough to land one on my own; but most of the time I would end up getting my line tangled on a tree branch or bush and have to wait for Dad to untangle and rethread my entire pole.

By the time I hit my teen years, I had lost interest in fishing altogether. Dad had purchased a home on a piece of property with a bubbling brook bordering its south perimeter. There was a quiet spot just downstream where the small tributary came to a calm, and the only noise was the symphony of insects serenading in the nearby brush. It was Dad's own little slice of heaven. Several times he tried to persuade me to join him for an impromptu afternoon of fishing. But I chose to spend time with my friends, unaware of just how precious and fleeting our time together would become.

This past summer, my husband and I took our three sons to a local park for a picnic. There was a small man-made pond for fishing, and we thought it might be a fun opportunity for the boys to give it a try. It had been twenty-five years since I had picked up a fishing pole.

It was a pleasant surprise to know that my reintroduction to the sport was a lot like riding a bike. It took a few minutes to find that familiar rhythm and timing, but before I knew it, that feeling of comfort and ease found in something visited before began to envelop me. I began to instruct my son Jack using the same words my dad had used to instruct me.

I could feel Jack's eyes follow each of my steady movements, as I cast out the line and reeled it in, and back out again, each cast determined to find just the right spot. The sound of his voice broke the silence between us.

"How did you learn so much about fishing?" he asked. I felt my eyes begin to well up and was grateful to have my sunglasses to hide behind.

"I learned from my dad," I told him.

Jack turned toward me and we both smiled. Then we turned our attention back in the direction of the water. The quiet calm between us felt nice as we stood side by side on the embankment and watched the afternoon sun glistening off the water's smooth surface. I smiled to myself. I was in no hurry for this moment to pass, as together we waited with patience for our first big catch.

———◆———

MICHELE RUVALCABA has found inspiration in putting her pen to paper since childhood. She has published both personal essays and poetry, and she is an active member of Southern California *Word Weavers* writing group. She lives in Ladera Ranch with her husband and three sons and is currently working on a collection of essays as well as her memoirs. Another story by this author appears in the Encore section of this anthology.

Letter from Cousin Amanda

My dearest Warren,

I trust my FedEX note (no E-Mail for this female Methuselah) will find you well, productive and enjoying your life and work. I am getting along as well as can be expected for one who has watched more decades come and go than I dare count.

My purpose for answering your recent missive straightaway is to introduce a twice-removed cousin, Mai Monet, who will be vacationing in Hong Kong next month. I would appreciate whatever courtesies you can extend to her at that time.

You and Mai share a number of common interests which, if nourished, could blossom into a meaningful friendship, from which a contented bachelor and a care-free bachelor-ette might both benefit.

I have on numerous occasions attempted to arrange a rendezvous between the two of you, but to no avail. Mai has artfully thwarted my efforts. Therefore, my only recourse is to choose an underhanded method to stage an introduction, namely a letter from me to be hand delivered to you by Mai.

Please excuse my impudence and Mai's abbreviated skirt, boots and independent nature. Instead I suggest you acquaint yourself with one of the most delightful, exciting and exasperating daughters of Eve ever to cross Buddha's path.

My best wishes to your honorable family.

Expectantly yours,

Amanda

P.S. Please do keep me advised.

***

Three weeks later, before Dr. Warren Lew's office hours began, his desk nurse announced the day's first call.

"Good morning," a male voice, professional but friendly, answered after a brief silence.

"Lucky for him," I mumbled. I detest having to listen to a ringing phone.

"Dr. Warren Lew?" I pronounced the three words as one.

"This is Dr. Lew speaking."

Hmm! It was a minor shock that Amanda's old crony didn't sound nearly as prehistoric as her Los Angeles colony of ancients.

"Dr. Lew, my name is Mai Monet and I'm calling on behalf of my cousin, Amanda Yee."

"Good morning, Miss Monet. Amanda informed me you would call during your visit. And how is my dear friend?"

I had neither time nor patience to waste on a lengthy conversation about my overbearing cousin twice-removed and forty-seven years my senior. Therefore, in as few words as possible, I explained that Amanda had written him a letter and insisted I personally present it before returning home.

We arranged to meet that evening in the main lobby of the Peninsula Hotel. While dressing for my last night of Hong Kong pleasures, I felt my blood pressure registering above one hundred and seventy over ninety. Dear old Cousin Amanda, always using her matriarchal rank to get her way. How unreasonable. How dare she infringe on my good nature and precious time to deliver her ridiculous letter to a stranger, possibly a former lover.

I arrived my customary thirty minutes late and immediately looked about for my cousin's geriatric friend. Business people, foreign visitors, ladies of pleasure

40

and hotel personnel streamed back and forth between the Salisbury Road entrance, the registration desk, boutiques and crowded elevators.

No one appeared to be looking for me, only at me. Men lifted eyebrows and smiled. Their female companions quickly steered them in an opposite direction. My one hundred seven pounds under a body-hugging sequined tee shirt and spandex skirt produced the usual lustful stares, but I, of course, didn't notice.

Where is Dr. Lew and why isn't he here waiting for me? I pouted. I had already shortened my night's activities by one hour and agonized over every lost minute. Reluctantly I seated myself on a cushioned sofa and eyed my surroundings.

The Peninsula's lobby furnished with tables of glossy dark woods, silk shaded lamps, comfortable chairs and couches invited all who crossed its threshold to partake of the famed hotel's hospitality. However, after minutes of partaking, I grew antsy and breathed fire. I will wait only a minute more, I swore, then leave and concoct a little white lie to tell Amanda as an excuse for not delivering her damned letter.

At this point I realized I wasn't the only one waiting for someone. A gentleman, from head to toe, sat across from me on the other side of a carved rosewood table. He was neither too young nor above the age that invited a second look, which I willingly gave as he anxiously examined every face that passed before him.

I tried, but couldn't avoid noticing the forest green velvet suit, dreary tie and unfashionable camel hair topcoat neatly folded across his lap. His wardrobe was terribly dated and tastefully ugly. "Ugh," I mouthed. Anyone so out of touch with good taste certainly deserves to be kept waiting – all night at the very least.

As though I had spoken aloud, my co-watcher glanced at me, nodded and checked his Rolex. For more than twenty minutes, he with polite endurance and I on the brink of volcanic action, played the waiting game seeking faces that were seeking ours.

Silently cursing the unknown Dr. Lew, Amanda and myself for being her respectful puppet, I swore if the anonymous doctor didn't make an appearance within the next sixty seconds, I would leave the bothersome letter with the Night Manager. All of a sudden, the green suit looked directly at me with an all too familiar gleam in his eye.

"My humble apologies for intruding upon your thoughts, Madam, but as it appears we both might be victims of ailing watches, unforeseen accidents or forgetfulness; perhaps I may be of some assistance."

I started to leave without comment, but a strange sensation held me captive and I found myself responding to his courtesy with the story of my mission and the anger I felt toward my dowager kin and her distrust of the overseas mail system.

The handsome face above the velvet admitted he, too, was meeting an elderly visitor from America. "As I must await my unknown guest, I will be most happy to assume the responsibility of delivering your letter or deposit it with the concierge if the addressee has not arrived when I must leave. And perhaps your schedule will permit me to enjoy an after dinner drink with you later this evening?" he asked hopefully.

"I'm afraid that would be quite impossible. I have plans for the remainder of this night and tomorrow I catch an early flight for Los Angeles. But thank you for the invitation, Mr, uh—?"

"Lew, Dr. Warren Lew and may I have the pleasure of knowing to whom I am speaking?"

My stomach cartwheeled. Shock diluted with a large dose of chagrin rendered me mute for one of the rare times in my life. Dr. Lew patiently repeated his question.

"Your old friend's cousin," I replied with the ingrained courtesy and age-old charm of many generations of well-bred female ancestry. All the while a nagging thought took shape and erupted into a flash of irritation. Cousin Amanda really should have been more persistent in her efforts to introduce the good doctor to me long ago. After all, wardrobes can be updated.

———◆●◆———

JOY BLANK is a long-time member of the Orange Coast Writers and the Writer's Circle based in San Juan Capistrano. A resident of Laguna Niguel, she writes fiction, Haiku, and essays. Previously published in *Interstices: the Orange County Anthology*, she is currently completing her first novel and a collection of short stories. Another story by this author appears in the Encore section.

Anyone who says they have only one life to live must not know how to read a book.

—Author Unknown

PATRICIA DREYFUS

Renovation

The workman arrives,
leather tool belt
jangles behind me
as we walk to the window
he came to repair.

On my desk scattered
books and papers
divert his attention.
"What do you do?"
"I'm a writer, a poet."

He tests the window cracks
with swollen fingers,
walks outside, inspects
casing and glass.

He slides open the
fractured window,
his ruddy face
framed in space.

Eyes glance up,
he blinks, looks
quickly down.
"I wrote a poem once.
Want to hear it?"

"Yes of course."
The polite reply.
"It's in the style of
Emily Dickenson."

He looks directly at me
assembles, caresses
every word, every line,
repairing, restoring the day.

❖

Lesson in Living

So that's the way
it's going to be,

she declared,
never dropping
her gaze.

It was the doctor
who looked away.

But not today, her
azure eyes shouted.

Each day,
as always,
began with prayer.

She dressed,
put on lipstick,
gathered friends.

Not today,
she announced,

squarely facing
the young priest
full of trite consolation.

Not today,
she whispered,

as her halo
of white hair
fell in her hands.

❖

Sailing at Lake Tahoe

Her mouth, an imploded cave
under a knobbed nose,
cheeks embarrassed by rouge,
a yellowed apple doll face
etched by fissures that run
like mountain creeks.

Her eyes, incisions,
embedded holes
in sandy dunes.
Hair, singed dark
like dried seaweed
on the shore.

Listing side to side,
an ancient battleship,
she sails steadily forward,

balanced on the rudder
of a claw foot cane.

Her barnacled hand
anchors a chair.
A soft grunt,
hoists her stern,
onto the seat.

Cabled fingers
fish for a concealed
coffer. Finding fortune
she keels forward,
launches treasure
into the slot.

Second Opinion

"Well, how are we, Young Lady?" He smiled, the corners of his lips curling up over the ends of a sparse gray mustache.

I had been waiting nearly an hour in the winter white exam room, my right knee aching. We? I thought. Young Lady? I'm sixty-two and-a-half. Is he talking to me?

"I hear we have a little sore knee." He grinned. He was starched, stiff in a crisp three-quarter-length, long-sleeved white smock. His eyes were pale blue, his hair a gray cap on his head. He looked like a very anemic version of the doctor on the old "Love Boat" series.

Smirking, he patted the exam table. "Do you think we can jump up here?" I wanted to throw my arms around his neck and shout "Let's!" But I controlled my urge and got "us" up on the table.

The doctor put the MRI I had brought with me on the light board. "Oh my." He shook his head. His brow furrowed. "We have a lot of arthritis on the tibia, and in ten years we could have bone necrosis and the whole bone could die."

Is this guy real? I thought. "Doctor Carry," I said, "I would rather deal with why my leg aches now than with what may or may not happen in ten years."

"Of course," he replied.

"I think I injured my knee riding my exercise bicycle," I explained. The smile arched again.

"Biking's not for us." He grinned. I began to look around the room for hidden cameras. Surely this was a bad joke.

Undaunted and wanting an answer, I continued, "I walk three miles twice a week and lately my knee hurts so badly I can't finish."

"Walking's not for us," said the doctor, shaking his head. Did he really say that again? Couldn't be. I thought my children or several of my sneaky friends would set something like this up. Where are the cameras?

I tried to salvage the visit. "I do water aerobics three times a week and my knee hurts then too."

"Oh, the water's for us," he said, seeming very satisfied with this pronouncement. I just stared at him. I didn't know whether to laugh or cry.

"My knee hurts in the water too, Dr. Carry. You are listed as specializing in sports medicine. What can I do?"

He turned and walked, head down, toward the other side of the room, seemingly deep in thought. "Well," said Dr. Carry from his perch on a high stool against the wall, the word coming out as a sigh, "as I see it, there are three things we can do. We can have surgery, although I don't think it will do us any good. We can have an injection of a lubricant that is made from rooster combs. Or," and this seemed to delight him, "we can just go home, sit down, and take it easy."

Was this a proposal from a man I had just met? We were now one. He was planning "our" life and the options weren't good. I didn't want to go home and sit down. I had a lot to do.

Still trying to stay focused and hoping for some relief, I asked, "How long have they been using the rooster comb injection?"

"About five years," he replied.

"So you don't know the long term effects?" I questioned.

"Oh," he oozed, the smile bending, "we don't have to worry about long term effects."

I wanted to grab my throat or his and shout, "How long do WE have?"

I persisted. I was not going to let "us" get discouraged. I told him, "I used to teach tennis and loved it. I was hoping to get back to the game."

"Tennis is not for us," sang Dr. Carry. "But," he added, seemingly pleased with himself, "the ball is in your court."

"Oh Lord," I moaned inwardly. "Not bad clichés too?"

As he began to back out of the door, he said, "Now, just let us know what we want to do." What "we" want to do, I thought, is never, ever see your face or hear about "us" again. We, us, you and I are finished!

I limped out of the office, furious, leg aching, got into my car and burst into tears. Did he even hear what he told me? What rotten choices. My active life was over.

Then I thought about the supercilious Dr. Carry and "our" visit and I began to laugh. I laughed and laughed.

Another surgeon has since fixed "our" knee and last week "we" played tennis. But Doctor Carry and I are forever joined in mirth. In fact, every time I think about "us," I laugh even though "we" will never meet again.

PATRICIA DREYFUS is an award-winning poet and freelance writer with five children and eleven grandchildren. She's a member of *The Writing Well*, *Pen American Center*, and the *Greater Los Angeles Writers Society*.

The future belongs to those who believe in the beauty of their dreams.

– Eleanor Roosevelt

MARY ANNE BALMUTH

Dublin Days

A lifetime of imagining
and he brings me here
to wander by the River Liffey
where a barge makes its way down dark waters.
We wend our way among pedestrians
who pause to steal a wee glance at the grand scene
before hurrying by.
We stroll
over a foot bridge
where lovers linger
tow-headed tykes race
and the sky stretches out before us,
gray as the stone buildings in the distance,
ripe with the smell of more rain
and we don't care.

My grandfather walked these streets once,
A farm boy visiting the city,
A young man squandering his last Irish days
before boarding a boat to a better life.
I see his face in the people we pass:
fair skin, blue eyes,
white-haired old men like the grandpa he became
years later
across the sea.

On Grafton Street, we sip tea in an outdoor café,
savor the scent of lilies wafting by,
and then we join the crowds again,

browsing through shop displays,
splashing through the soft rain,
marching to the beat of a fiddler's jig
that follows us down the street.

❖

Reunion

A hundred faces fill the corridor,
pounding feet,
rolling suitcases.
I search for only one
compact figure
with a backpack,
sparkling eyes that find my own.
The glass door slides open and

You are here,
ushering in sunshine,
crescendos,
relief.

"It was amazing,"
you whisper as we embrace.
"Epic."
"Life-changing."
Stories pour out as we walk,
but I hear only two things:

You are safe.
You are home.

❖

The Game

(Anthem of a Lakers Fan)

"Let the game come to you,"
the mantra says.
"Be in the moment."
And so they pass the ball around,
looking for the play,
the move,
the opening.
And when everything is working
they soar above the rest,
propel the orb on a rainbow arc
that sends it through the net.
Or one teammate finds another,
revels in the thunderous finish.
Or a player makes his own path,
finds redemption with the softest touch.

And sometimes they miss the mark.
The ball clanks hard,
bounces long.
They dive to corral the prize,
but it skitters.
They scramble after it,
but the possibility bounces away.

But still we roar –
"Get the rebound!"
"Get the ball!"
"Shoot, shoot, shoot!"
And they fight and push and fake,
leap to make the play,
leave gravity behind
and take our breath away

And we stand
when they win and when they lose,
For
they are warriors
and they are champions
and they are people who we'll never be,
who bound high
above the ordinary or difficult,
who carry us
while we leave the world behind
for just a little while,
and they are people just like us,
who stretch and strive,
who celebrate each victory when it comes,
who play the game when all is lost
until the last second drains away.

MARY ANNE BALMUTH has been a writer and editor for many years, contributing numerous articles about parenting, youth sports, theatre and childhood autism to Orange County's *Parenting Magazine, Sesame Street Parents, Welcome Home Magazine* and many other publications. She currently tutors third and fourth graders through the Saddleback Valley School District's No Child Left Behind program and is working on completing a mystery novel.

JESIKAH MARIA ROSS

The Road to Yei

I'll admit, I never really imagined going to Sudan. Flying into Juba, the capital of the South, I catch my first glimpse of the place. It's what I'd imagined: vast expanses of open space with red dirt and scrub brush for as far as the eye can see. No people, no buildings, no sign of life as I know it. As we approach the tarmac I get a better visual on the city, a wild mix of run down old buildings, shiny new development, and thatched roof mud huts.

It's weird, albeit great, to be back in Africa. I'm here to give training on how to use media —video, radio, photography — as a tool for youth and community development. I've been brought over by WarChild, a non-governmental organization working to empower youth in war-torn areas to improve their lives through creative methods — like community-produced media, my specialty. I'll be working with the WarChild staff, their community partners, and a group of youth.

While I feel uncomfortable being a white American working in an impoverished area of Africa, I can't think of another thing that would bring me to the south of Sudan, and I'm grateful for the opportunity to get outside my comfort zone and experience this part of the world. If I'm able to contribute to a positive change for the masses of people caught up in Sudan's 23-year civil war, I'll feel it's well worth the time and effort.

Day two starts out innocently enough. At 6:00 a.m., I get a wakeup call, a cold shower, and a steaming cup of Nescafe. Of the three, the hardest part by far is the Nescafe. Our driver is on time, something I find somewhat astounding for Africa. At 7:30 a.m. on the dot we leave Juba. Our goal is to make it to Yei Town by noon, giving me two full hours to decompress and set up for the first day of the community media training. Yei is a small city about 100 miles from Juba on the road to Uganda, so four and a half hours seems do-able.

The first hour goes by well enough. The pavement ends about 30 minutes into the journey and we forge ahead on pretty decent dirt roads – the kind of jeep road throughout California's Sierra Nevada: plenty wide and well-packed with sprinkles of potholes that are easy to navigate. I'm thankful since I've taken the backseat of the Range Rover, which isn't really a seat but a fold down bench with no arms, minimal back support, and metal objects behind the slight back padding.

About 45 minutes in, I get clear on why it takes a long time to get down this road. For the next hour we negotiate the deepest holes, gouges, and slices of earth that I've ever traversed in a large, slow-moving, vehicle. My body experiences the kind of shake, rattle, and roll that I can only hope never to go through again.

Bracing myself with my feet AND hands, I jolt up and down, side to side, and backward and forward – not necessarily in that order and usually in combination. As you might surmise, I'm starting to wonder what the hell I was thinking when I told WarChild: "Sure, I'd love to come do a training in Southern Sudan." I'm trying to put on a good face and make it all seem normal and no big deal while inside I'm cursing myself for leaving the cushiness of the USA and my humble job at a university. My neck is starting to feel muscles I didn't know existed, and my head is starting to realize that the only defense I've had against this whole ordeal so far is a bloody cup of Nescafe.

Fortunately, like most deeply painful moments, it does pass and 90 minutes later we are all of a sudden on a road that is quite nice. Or, maybe after that ANY road is quite nice. That's when we hit our first roadblock. They are de-mining in this area and when they are at work they shut down the roads. (Southern Sudan was filled with land mines during the civil war. The countryside is so rife with them that people can only use roads and designated paths to move around.) This is what my sponsors feared, as it can take anywhere from 45 to 90 minutes for these check points to open. Stopping, we hope for the best and suddenly realize how hot it can be in a Range Rover with the air conditioning turned off. Just when we start to drip (read: 5 minutes max) we luck out. The road is opened.

As we roll by the worksite, I see the United Nations' de-mining trucks. They look like something straight out of a sci-fi film: otherworldly in design and form. They resemble big mutant bugs with their long, cylindrical bodies on top of wide axles with extra fat wheels. I'm guessing that funky shape is useful when combing every centimeter of the uneven countryside to locate and remove mines safely.

About an hour later, we hit roadblock two. This time we aren't so fortunate and we get out of the car to try and find some shade under the tarp of an impromptu-looking outdoor shop offering water, fruit, and other snacks. Evidently, these entrepreneurial kiosks are set up daily where the de-mining is happening and do a good business with all the folks, like us, that are stranded in a hot, dusty place for longer than they want.

But again we luck out; only 15 minutes later the road opens. I'm incredibly thankful as I'm sopping wet with sweat and wondering just what kind of presence I'll be able to command at this training if I look like a drowned rat that has been coated from head to toe with red dust kicked up at the roadblocks.

We are so glib about our fortune. My colleague remarks how it's only 11:30 a.m. and we are just 30 minutes from our destination. She talks about how we'll enjoy a nice leisurely lunch and have everything in place before training participants arrive. She jinxes us. Maybe 30 seconds later, white smoke starts to pour in from the car vents. I think it's the air conditioning, probably a weird Freon clog that will pass in a second. But then it turns black and we know we are in trouble. We stop the car immediately, and I quickly grab our equipment out of the back. I know that type of smoke is not right and the smell is even more wrong.

The driver, sensing imminent danger, starts to pour water on the dashboard. I'm thinking, "shit, this guy just toasted the Range Rover; it was probably only a small electrical glitch." It turns out the whole area in front of the steering wheel is melting and catching fire, so he did the right thing.

Fortunately, the nice UN de-mining contractors come to our assistance. After 45 more minutes in the blazing sun and then 30 minutes driving painfully slowly in an un-air-conditioned second Rover, I reach my first destination at 1:15, 45 minutes before the training starts. I'm dripping with sweat, stink, and am suffering from a lack of bonafide caffeine. Worse, I'm starting to hit a jet lag wall. My head is too rattled from the whole series of sagas to think quickly or creatively. I'm starting to wonder if I'm going to pull off this first day of training.

I realize I need something to lift my spirits and reboot my addled brain. With nowhere else to turn, I envision Nescafe as my friend, my knight in shining armor (those who know me realize how incredibly visionary I need to become to really embrace this perspective). I wash up, grab a quick lunch, and swill down the biggest mug full of the elixir I can come up with. With 15 minutes to spare, I make my way to the training venue. Then I rock the first training session! We all have a blast, do some fun games and intros, and set a fantastic tone for the rest of the week.

Thank you, Nescafe!

————◆————

JESIKAH MARIA ROSS is a media artist who works with schools, non-governmental organizations and social action groups around the globe to create participatory projects that generate media literacy, civic engagement, and community change. She's the principal of Praxis Projects (www.praxisprojets.net) and the founding director of the *Art of Regional Change* program at the University of California, Davis.

NANCY KLANN

The Lois and Clark Affair

Her husband was out of town on a business trip, and rather than drive home to an empty house after work, she went to Prima Pasta, one of the many bistros that dotted the coast highway. A typical spot, where straw covered Chianti bottles sat on the tables and paintings from local artists covered the walls.

She didn't go there to eat, but she still enjoyed the magnetic scent of garlic and herbs that followed her into the bar next to the dining room. After she positioned herself on the barstool, the man to her left began speaking to her. His head bobbed and his words came out in high-pitched chirps. A thick accent made him difficult to understand, but she gathered his mother had been a frail woman and recently fallen quite ill. She half-listened out of politeness, but her eyes turned away when she'd had enough of his gloomy conversation.

A man with an easy, open smile caught her attention. He had a boyish face that triumphed over his grey-flecked hair. Creases ran from his nose to the outside of his full lips. He wore a yellow cardigan, tortoiseshell glasses, and a wedding band. There was an empty stool to her right, separating them.

He was talking with a bearded man in a blue and white seersucker suit. He smoked on a plastic cigarette with an LED light at the tip, and it glowed with each inhale. She took a big gulp of scotch and noticed that the appealing man had turned toward her, with an ambushed expression.

"You've got to help me," he said. "May I move over next to you?"

"Please, yes. I could use a little help myself."

They collided, bumping heads as he shifted to move over.

"My name is Clark."

Her dark hair fell forward and covered her lean face as she reached to shake his hand. "Clark, you're not going to believe this, but my name is Lois. Did you come here to save me?" She instantly wished those lame-brained words hadn't escaped from her mouth.

"Maybe we saved each other."

He was the first man named Clark she had ever met, and it seemed like an invitation to something – something exclusive. Lois Lane had been much more than a fictional character to her when she was young. She had been, well, real. Every time she saw a "Superman" rerun on the family television, she watched Clark Kent save and protect Lois – unconditionally.

Her affinity toward Lois Lane was dreamy and had to do with her – *their* – destinies as well as their names. Just like the leading lady on the television, she knew her Prince Charming would be named Clark.

Over twenty years later, in the instant it took him to say his name, she was seized with expectation. He hailed from Omaha; he chatted about a recent rafting trip down the Colorado River and ordered Bombay Sapphire gin. He liked to play golf as often as possible and didn't like the government requiring him to fasten his seat belt. She could smell a distant hint of juniper when he put his hand on her arm. His touch was firm and warm on her skin and reached deep into the nerve endings that danced with anticipation, as if emerging from a fallout shelter after years of isolation.

She felt her mood climb in the direction of the future, like a seed sprouting toward an artificial stimulus. A buoyant part of her that had been tucked away broke free in animated gestures and deep, throaty laughs. Her cheeks became ruddy. She was a carnal desert in need of a heavy rain.

Lois didn't talk about her profession, colleagues, or research projects. Her husband wasn't mentioned. Instead, she told Clark some of the soft things about herself. About her love of modern art and the ballet, and how when crossing bridges, she still believed there might be a troll lurking underneath. She described her favorite beach, complete with sandpipers dancing with the tides. Clark said he liked the way her eyes greeted laughter willingly and that her whole face smiled when she talked, then he checked his watch.

"Have you had dinner?"

"I had a late lunch. I guess I'm drinking my dinner."

"Please, keep me company. Let's get a table and have something to eat."

The table was private. Close to a corner fireplace and far from the kitchen noise. A neglected log had burned out, and carried the scent of smoldering intimacy. Their surroundings narrowed to the confines of two, and somehow, very quickly narrowed more. Her head was pulsing to the rhythm of fantasy. She called forth imaginary characters from the city of Metropolis and placed them at the table.

They talked of music and favorite cities. They decided, together, that croutons and strawberries were overrated because you have to eat too many to find a good one. She became flush from her reverie and absorbed with the idea of Lois and Clark, fate and magic, and being taken care of forever.

Busboys cleared the surrounding tables as she talked once more about her favorite beach.

"Why don't we get out of here and do something together?" he said.

"That sounds great."

"How about a walk on that beach of yours?"

She wasn't sure how they got there, but they were there, wrapped in a surreal mist, walking barefoot. It was a sheltered cove not far from the restaurant. She had walked along that shore often in daylight, but nightfall stretched the dark cliffs and amplified the rhythmic waves that pounded with urgency.

With the first kiss, the surf ran carelessly over their feet and, without warning, rushed up their legs. Then it fled back to the ocean and played with undercurrents of desire and illusion. Lois and Clark stayed there, saturated in themselves for hours.

In Clark's hotel room, with its artificial plants and reproduced artwork, she felt strangely safe – the way it feels when looking at faded photographs of unknown relatives. She could have been in a fortress like the ones in make-believe stories.

She paid for their night together with pockets full of denial, and made love between sips of champagne in a blue-stemmed glass. In bed, he touched her with whispers. She listened and permitted herself to savor her recklessness.

With an innocent stroke of his hand, the stone on Clark's wedding ring caught and pulled on the locket that hung from her neck. A picture of her husband was inside. The chain ripped the smooth flesh of her neck. She lay there, startled in an aroused emptiness. Darkness hid the blood that congealed on her neck and heightened the irony of their separate declarations of fidelity.

She was naked, fragile, and restless, on a bed turned coarse and soiled. She imagined a scar forming on her neck. A scar that would require concealer.

When dawn broke through the opening between the hotel drapes, she turned on her side and stared at his back. There was a galaxy of freckles and dark moles and secrets before her. It looked like a human dot-to-dot puzzle with no numbers to help make sense of it. The place of her fantasy had vanished, with no eyewitnesses, no police reports, and no clause for that kind of casualty on any of her insurance policies.

He turned over and sleepily said, "Last night was wonderful."

She reached up past the locket and stroked her neck. She thought about Kryptonite and desire, and had to laugh at herself for confusing Clark with Superman.

NANCY KLANN has received numerous awards for her writing. She was a finalist in two *Glimmer Train* short story contests. She received the *Best Unpublished Short Story* award as well as a finalist honor at the San Diego Book Awards and holds *Excellence in Writing* awards from the Santa Barbara Writers Conference. Her Encore story that appears in this anthology received the *First Place Award* in the San Diego Book Awards.

ELAINE PIKE

Riding the Carousel

My Journalism 101 professor was a guy by the name of Larry Mott. A tall mast of a man, Larry loomed at 6 foot 6. He preferred Larry to Professor Mott, and he ran a casual ship. Larry fought in Vietnam, where he suffered an injury as the result of a parachute accident. All he could say about it was, "Overshot my landing target and got tangled in the trees." We later found out that they were being fired upon as they dropped, and Larry barely escaped with his life. Consequently, he walked with a limp in his step and was plagued with continual back pain. He often stood to address the class, pacing, while he twirled the ends of his handlebar mustache.

"There are many facets of journalistic study," he began. "Since this is an intro class, it is my aim to cover the craft as thoroughly as possible, within the confines of the semester." My eyes followed him back and forth as he paced. "In journalism, you will discover your passion." He fixed a serious gaze upon us, surveying the young faces of the nine men and three women in the room.

"Through journalism, you will seek verifiable fact. For journalism, you will strive to uncover truth. And by journalism, you will make a difference in the world." His voice rose with every line, accentuating each proposition. By sheer height alone, Larry cast a commanding presence. I anxiously flipped through the syllabus in my lap, curious to uncover his agenda. Our first assignment was due by the next class meeting — observe an on-campus student gathering, whether it be speech, rally, protest, music, sports event or any other qualifying newsworthy public display, and document the observation in no more than 500 words. Undaunted, I remember thinking "piece of cake" as we parted for the afternoon, never suspecting how this assignment would forever change the course of my life.

And the reason it changed the course of my life was this: I wrote an article entitled "Their Pain Alone" that had been influenced by a small gathering in the quad the following day. Two men addressed the participants in Spanish. I wandered to the edge of the circle amazed by what I heard. My brother and I had spent summers in Peru, among the native Quechua people, yet I had never considered their way of life to be anything less than my own; different, yes, but never beneath me. I had been raised to respect other cultures, embracing the differences, and acknowledging diversity with an observant, yet unbiased eye. That afternoon, I discovered a shocking truth; there were governments that murdered people in condemnation of their status in life, a chilling fact to an American girl like me who was raised on a promise and a smile.

I squeezed my books tightly in my arms, swaying on my feet at the edge of the circle. The dozen or so participants gripped posters bearing curly-edged photographs of the missing or dead — the date of disappearance memorialized beneath each name. A chill washed over me as the speakers enunciated the names, "Maria Teresa Gallegos. Juan Miguel De Santos. Julio Obregon. Gonzalo Jorge Medina," trading off from one name to the next with a purposeful rhythm. Fourteen names in all, recited in the beat of a dirge, until the last — a long pause emphasizing the somber moment.

"This afternoon, we gather to honor our brothers, sisters, mothers, fathers, and friends who chose to stand up and fight against the injustice. Consider this: basic human rights are in jeopardy. Land ownership, education and healthcare are the hostages of a greedy, ruthless government seeking to destroy basic human rights."

"A disgrace, una desgracia!" someone shouted.

"Dignity for all!" declared a young woman in the crowd, and the others followed suit.

"Dignidad para todos!" they chanted.

"Innocent lives have been violated by a philosophy," the second protestor continued as the crowd settled down. He raised a poster bearing the photograph of a young woman who looked nearly my age. I couldn't take my eyes off the photo depicting the serious countenance of a young girl, eyes reflecting like dark mirrors. "The government strives to keep wealth in the hands of the wealthy and out of the hands of the poor."

"To accomplish their goal," the first man declared, picking up the thread, "they have enacted a murderous reign of terror." The word terror, enunciated in Spanish, sent a powerful wave through the crowd. Angry tirades were simultaneously carried away on the breeze of a chill afternoon.

"The oppressed have risen in an attempt to quell the onslaught. These faces," he said with an eerie calm, gesturing with open palms like a supplicant poised in prayer, "represent the proud citizens who have put their lives on the line for justice."

"Justicia!" a woman decreed, reiterating the bold lettering on her poster.

The speaker's voice rose in a passionate plea. "They have courageously joined in a struggle against the government to maintain dignity and human rights while at the same time risking their lives."

"Power to the people!" someone shouted, clenched fist raised high, the cry echoing among the participants in the circle. Clenching my own fists in empathetic anger, I turned and walked away.

I was floored. My father had spent countless years in Central America excavating ruins, yet he had failed to mention any of this to us. Governments, good or bad, were rarely discussed around our dinner table. My father disliked political agendas, being a geek in every sense of the word. We would discuss science, archaeological finds, historical events, even philosophy, but no words were spoken to reveal atrocities such as these.

A twinge of betrayal crept over me, as if he had purposely withheld information to protect me from the ugly truth. As soon as I returned to my apartment, I picked up the telephone and called him, nonchalantly relaying the details of my journalism class to him, and describing the upcoming assignment. Then the conversation shifted as I recounted the events of the rally, asking, "Pop, how come you never told us? All those years you spent down there, and you never mentioned a thing!" My voice was shaky, overcome with emotion that was hard to mask.

And his reply, so typical of my Pop, was, "Because you never asked." Short and sweet and as non-committal as it could be. As if my lack of inquisitiveness was a reason to defer the harsh reality. His work and subsequent travels took him far to the north of the turmoil, and his primary focus centered on chalked, twelve-inch sections of dirt. "We couldn't let the brutality of the times interfere with our work, Rosie. We were part of a big picture, a team, loyal to teamwork and responsibility. Together, working toward a common goal. Excavation and discovery! And yes, the civil war raged while we dug. Lives were lost, an unpleasant reality, undeniably so. But we couldn't take our eyes off the project, didn't take our eyes off it, in the thick of the jungle, while the drama played out around us."

He left me speechless on the phone, my mind racing for a response. "Sometimes, Rosie," he said quietly, "it's easier that way. Focus on your work, while the world spins around you." That was my Pop. Honest to a fault, and faithful to his work. His honesty soothed my anger and calmed my sense of betrayal. I understood, but I also believed that this was the first time in my life, in all of my twenty years, that I tasted the bitter pill of reality. In spite of the shortcomings I had experienced, in spite of the unpleasant difficulties I had lived through, nothing compared to the downtrodden expressions on the faces of those students at the rally. It was their sense of sorrow, their furrowed brows and desperate voices that instigated a pivotal turn in my life.

———◆———

ELAINE PIKE made a journal entry on June 10, 1970: "I am trying to write a book." Forty years later, she participates in *Saturday Mornings Coffee & Critique* and is diligently working on *Riding the Carousel*, a fictional account of a girl struggling with forgiveness. Another sample of this author's work appears in the Encore section.

Farie Momayez

Waiting

I sit in darkness
waiting for a light.
I compromise.
How about a shadow,
a bird flying by,
a leaf moving?
Like a whirling dervish
I spin,
hoping for a light.
Alas, no bird flies by,
no leaf is turned,
and no high,
no light.
Only the dot of darkness prevails.

The Eyes of a Lover

Your gentle eyes follow me
from side to side.
Did the ghost of Da Vinci create this scene?
I see a world of approval, love and hope
in those large brown eyes.
My body aches to touch you.
Those eyes have followed me
for a thousand and one years.
Only now
they are trapped behind glass
on a large frame
forever untouchable.

The Sounds of Joy

Driving the distance to see our kids
I reach to hold
who I hope quietly sits
Invisible, your soft
flesh like flannel.
I touch the dial,
change the channel
AM to FM,
no sad sounds of the blues
no preaching
no news.
Joy is my choice
MJ with his immortal voice
makes my fingers
dance to the band.
The dashboard takes
the place of your hand.

FARIE MOMAYEZ, Ph.D., is a psychotherapist and life coach. Born in Iran, she was sent abroad as a teen by her parents who wanted to get her away from her boyfriend. A few years later, Parviz followed her to California; they were in love for 47 years before he died. She uses writing as a therapeutic outlet and is in the process of writing her memoir.

Kristin Orloff

September, 1982

Note: On the last night of the Military World Wrestling Championships in Venezuela, Reza grips his gold medal, knowing American wrestlers wait minutes away to help him defect. He must choose between his own freedom and the possible revenge killing of his thirteen-year-old brother, Hassan, locked in Ayatollah Khomeini's prison. In the following passage, his mother and two sisters visit Hassan in prison after Reza has defected.

Thursday. Soraya and Pari begged the principal to let them leave school thirty minutes early. After promises for additional study, they were allowed to leave.

The girls, carefully covered in chador, took the long bus ride to the prison and met their mother standing in line. Pari rushed to her side, clasped her hand, and held it tight. Inch by inch, they moved forward. Once at the front, they were ushered into a waiting room with rows of booths separated by thick sheets of dirty glass. Mostafa had arranged for Hassan to be transferred to this less brutal section of the prison and now the visits were conducted through a phone in each booth.

"Why did the line stop?" Pari whispered to Soraya. "Can you see what is happening?"

Soraya craned her neck. "It is the mother, two in front of us. The guard cannot find her son."

Nimtaj gently closed her eyes. Soraya and Pari gripped her hands, but they all remained silent. They would not look into each other's faces, for there, the truth would be written. Once Reza defected, no one was safe.

Holding a small pile of dirty clothes, a guard approached the waiting woman. She looked at the bundle and screamed for the dead. Her fists pounded on the guard as she damned them all to hell. He dropped the clothes and dragged her toward the door. In a moment, she was gone. Her cries echoing in the mothers' hearts, the small corpse of clothes lay untouchable. Another guard scooped it up and took it away.

Pari's sweaty hands trembled. Soraya struggled so hard to stop her tears that she forgot to breathe and the room began to spin. Only Nimtaj did not waver. She kept her head high and her eyes fixed on the row of booths.

Nimtaj approached the guard. "Hassan Abedi," she said.

He looked at his clipboard. He flipped a page. And then another. He tapped on the paper. Turning to another page, he paused.

Lifting her face to look directly into his, Nimtaj repeated, "Hassan Abedi."

Without looking up, his dirty fingernails turned through crinkled papers.

Pari squeezed her mother's hand and Soraya rubbed her fingers along her neck. In the awful silence, they waited.

Without looking up, the guard pointed. "Third," he said.

The girls scurried ahead of their mother and pressed their palms against the glass. Hassan's hand met theirs and he smiled. His eyes went to his mother and he nodded the "I'm okay Naneh" he gave every time she came.

Soraya reached for the phone and Hassan picked up his end. The news that they had come to share suddenly seemed frightening. What if he hears it as his death sentence? What if he curses and hates his brother?

Nimtaj lifted the phone. "My son," she said, "you are well?"

"I'm strong Naneh, yes," he said. But his gaze followed Soraya and Pari who looked away.

"Naneh," he said. "What is it? What's going on?"

"Reza," she said, then she gave the phone to Soraya.

"Oh no," Hassan said. "Did he lose in the championship?"

72

The phone trembled in Soraya's hand. Her lips parted but with no sound.

"What?" Hassan said.

"He's—," Soraya looked into Hassan's wary eyes. "He's not coming home."

Hassan's face criss-crossed with questions. "Not coming?"

"He escaped," she said. Tears spilled down her cheeks. "Ali, too."

Light sent her golden rays demanding darkness to yield. Hassan clenched his fists and shook them in victory while his lips repeated, "Reza is free. Reza is free."

KRISTIN ORLOFF is an assistant principal at a middle school and participates in *Saturday Mornings Coffee & Critique*. Based on the life of World Champion wrestler Reza Abedi, the above is an excerpt of a work in progress. http://iranianrootsamericanwings.blogspot.com

Breathe-in experience, breathe-out poetry.

– Muriel Rukeyse

JEANETTE A. FRATTO

The Rain in Spain Did Not Stay on the Plain
(and other unexpected events)

By the time our bus limped into the driveway of our hotel in Torremolinos, Spain, it resembled a MASH unit more than a tour bus of happy travelers. Almost half the occupants, including my husband, were in various stages of recovery from food poisoning, acquired the night before at our last hotel. Four people in our group were too sick to make the trip at all and remained behind under a doctor's care. Illness struck as we were about to begin our last week of a three-week adventure to Portugal and Spain. The first two weeks in Portugal had been wonderful, but as surely as the terrain from Portugal to Spain changed before our eyes, so did our fortunes.

Our last night in the lovely Algarve region gave no clue as to what would come. We dined sumptuously at the hotel buffet while trading stories of favorite places in Lisbon or Cascais. We eagerly anticipated traveling to Spain the next day, leaving by bus bright and early, 8 a.m. We headed to our rooms after dinner for last minute packing and early bed. By 11 p.m. our lights were out and I was curled up for a deep sleep, when I heard my husband stumbling to the bathroom. This was not unusual, but the sounds coming from the bathroom were. Never prone to nausea, my husband was now well into its throes. The bathroom visits continued hourly. By 6 a.m. he was weak but finally seemed to be over the worst. Gamely he prepared to be in shape to leave by 8 a.m. He even thought he could tolerate a light breakfast. He couldn't.

As we puzzled over what had gripped him, a knock on our door revealed he was not alone. The elderly couple next door had also spent the night developing a close relationship with the bathroom; they were still too ill to leave. They were waiting for the doctor and wanted us to inform the tour guide.

At breakfast it was clear the tour group had dwindled. Those who came to eat without their disabled spouses told similar stories of all night bathroom trips. This was not the ending we envisioned to our two weeks in Portugal.

As the bus pulled out at 8 a.m., minus four too sick to travel, it was a sorry affair. When we stopped for a chicken and rice lunch en route to Torremolinos, a special table was set up to serve hot tea and crackers to the ill. My husband joined them. Those of us who could eat did so guiltily.

By 4 p.m. we arrived at our hotel. I unpacked while my husband dived under the covers, not wanting to be disturbed until morning. I joined the few who were still well in the dining room for dinner. We hoped the next day would bring a positive change. Instead it brought rain.

We awoke early. My husband felt like his old self. We headed to the balcony of our 8th floor room to view the Mediterranean but saw only mist and fog. But it was early. Things would get better. After all, this was the Costa del Sol, and we were scheduled for a walking tour at 10 a.m.

We approached the dining room for breakfast, but instead of the smell of bacon and eggs, we were greeted by the smell and sight of water everywhere. A broken pipe in the kitchen had resulted in a flood. It seemed as if every hotel employee had a mop and a bucket for the clean-up effort. We were redirected to the upstairs cocktail lounge, where a makeshift continental breakfast had been set up. We joined our fellow travelers to muse over what would happen next. It didn't take long to find out.

By the time we gathered in the lobby for our walking tour, a light rain was falling. Our cheerful tour guide, Salvador, umbrella in hand, was rounding up the group while apologizing for the weather.

"Very unusual for this time of year," he kept repeating.

Undaunted by gathering storm clouds, Salvador headed for the outdoors with about 20 game travelers following behind. We circled around the hotel and into a charming street of shops and small hotels. The rain was now a steady downfall. Those who had umbrellas carried on. Those of us who didn't took shelter in a little shop, which just happened to have umbrellas on prominent display. We purchased one and kept going. By now we'd lost sight of Salvador and his merry group but were certain we'd find our way back. Our umbrella gave little protection. The wind was whipping as hard as the rain was falling, so everything from the knees down was soaked. Soggy and cold, we made it to our hotel room, changed into warm clothes, and contemplated our 2 p.m. bus tour to nearby Mijas.

The rain was still falling heavily when we boarded the bus. As we left Torremolinos, Salvador pointed out lovely landmarks we had to take on faith. The steamed windows and intense rain made visibility close to zero. When we reached Mijas, a torrent of muddy water cascaded near the main access road. Our driver maneuvered until he was able to pass through the ever-narrowing roadway and enter Mijas. Purported to be a charming town, Mijas was scheduled a 45-minute stop for shopping and sightseeing.

Everyone refused to leave the bus.

Salvador, not willing to give in so easily, promised that if anyone wanted to get off, we would have our stop. Group pressure prevailed. If anyone was brave enough to want to leave, they kept their silence. We quietly headed back to Torremolinos.

At our hotel we were greeted by darkness. A power failure had turned the hotel into a tomb. Disgruntled tourists were huddled in the lobby, including our recently returned couples from Portugal. Having recovered sufficiently, they took separate cabs to reach Torremolinos, at a cost of $400 each, cash only. Still smarting from that, they weren't happy about being stranded in a dark lobby with their luggage, unable to reach their rooms by elevator.

My husband and I climbed the eight floors to our room and wondered what dinner would be like. Cold food by candlelight? We were close. The hotel dining room, clean but damp from the morning flood, provided a buffet of cold food that we were hesitant to try. Could food poisoning strike twice on one trip? Sure, why not? Although light had been restored, it kept going out, leaving diners to grope for their plates until the next surge of power brought it back.

The next few days brought more rain than sun. Scheduled village tours were bravely attempted but not successful. Salvador, ever the optimist, proceeded with each day's plans as though we weren't having terrible weather. This, coupled with the hotel's inability to retain electrical power for more than a few hours at a time, made for a disappointing, if adventuresome, week.

On our final day in Torremolinos, my husband and I awoke to beautiful sunshine, blue skies, and full-blown head colds. The view from our room was breathtaking. We were determined to stroll the promenade along the Mediterranean, even though bed for the next 24 hours seemed much more appealing.

We strolled, snapped pictures, sucked cough drops, and lamented the timing of our visit. We were in a truly beautiful area, clearly evident on this brilliant day. Reluctantly we returned to our hotel to pack for the trip home.

As we headed to the Malaga airport at 6 am the next morning, it appeared that another beautiful day was dawning. Salvador implored us all to return again to the Costa del Sol. He knew we hadn't experienced it at its best. We watched through sleepy eyes as the city faded in the distance, pretty sure we'd give it another chance.

JEANETTE FRATTO bases much of her writing on her work experience. Her novels, *No Stone Unturned* and *No Good Deed*, feature a female probation officer. Winner of the *Writers Digest Annual Writing Competition* for both feature article and short story, she is a member of the Orange County Chapter of the *California Writers Club*.

Margie Hartford

Friends

I once knew a woman who had a dog she adored. The dog reached the age of fifteen and became sick. The woman was getting old, too, and her business was not doing too well either. She came to visit me for a few days and typed for me. I paid her and, after she returned home, I sent her a few hundred dollars more.

Her beloved dog grew feebler each day. Rather than see the animal suffer, my friend decided to put the dog down, a difficult decision. It cost her all of the money I gave her to do so. The dog truly had become her best friend.

Another woman I know owned a cat that in the old days would have been put to sleep. This cat had a leg amputated and needed a prosthisis. The woman however, lived on social security and the prosthisis would cost $6,000. Animals can be expensive and we grieve when we lose them. Even so, a four-legged friend is completely loyal and devoted.

A woman living alone feels more secure when walking with a dog. Dogs protect their owners and never leave our sides. Do we ever receive such devotion from humans?

Well, there's something to be said for human friends, and, in my opinion, having four or five close friends is best. If one can't be there for you, another will step in to help. My good friend Carolyn stayed a week after my husband's funeral to help me with all the details.

Years ago, in my twenties, I lived with a co-worker for a time and we helped each other. Dorothy confessed she was pregnant. She didn't want anyone to know, and for reasons of her own, didn't want to marry the father of her child. She offered to care for my little boy since I was newly divorced; she would cook, clean and amuse my boy and, in exchange, I would pay the rent and buy the food. Dorothy planned to put her baby up for adoption and get on with her life, but in the meantime she needed me and I needed her, and we became friends.

Extremely thoughtful, Dorothy often made cookies for people or sent cards. From her example, I learned to be thoughtful, too.

I helped out my Greek friend, Zov, who also found herself pregnant in a time when it would have been disastrous. She showed up at my real estate office and told me the news. "Margie, please help me, I don't know how to get an abortion in this country. My brother will kill me if he finds out."

I knew she was right; her brother would never let her forget her mistake. He had supported the family, moved them from Greece after the Korean War, and this was the seventies, after all.

I made a few phone calls and found an abortion clinic open on Sunday, the only day Zov had off. I sat in the waiting room for about an hour and a half until it was over. That's what friends do. A few years later, she married a man of her choice and the family was none the wiser. Friends are loyal, help one another, and keep secrets, too.

I have been very fortunate to have some long-time friends who have helped me, some with emotional support, others with creativity, and all have been loyal. Trust, understanding and mutual respect are what's needed in a true friend. To forget an obligation or be ungrateful for a kindness is not a way to treat a friend in my book.

The head of psychiatry at Stanford recently said, "Women connect with each other differently and provide support systems that help them deal with stress and difficult life experiences." Physically, this quality girlfriend time helps us create more serotonin—a neurotransmitter that helps combat depression and creates a general feeling of well-being. Women share feelings.

Nina was another friend from whom I learned creativity and sense of design, but her financial acumen left something to be desired. And there was her drinking.

She came into the house through the garden gate, looked around, and exclaimed, "The flowers look great, Margie. The garden is beautiful! Got any scotch?"

When I handed her a drink, she sat down at the kitchen table and started her usual lament about her children. She went on to say she hated her newly rented room in a house with a strange assortment of people. She confided that she liked the transvestite best because of his sense of humor and great companionship.

I met Nina at a party given by friends over forty years ago. A strikingly beautiful woman, she wore her long hair in a straight black bob and bangs. Tall, she had a flare and fashion sense displayed in the exotic clothes she liked to wear. Whenever Nina entered a room, she dominated it with the force of her personality. Her creativity in terms of art, dressing, knitting, and interior design was truly exceptional. Her sense of humor was delightful and child-like; she charmed everyone. Nina, however, had a back-story.

When people think of leaving money to relatives, they don't realize the consequences the gift may have. Nina's aunt left a trust fund of about $450,000 each to Nina and her brothers. The trust fund paid her a monthly allowance until age 55 when she was awarded the bulk payment.

She'd been advised by lawyers to hire an attorney and an accountant to help her. I told her to buy a house or condo near work and put the rest into savings. I'm afraid her great generosity was her undoing. She gave her adult son and daughter large amounts of her inheritance to pay off their bills.

Nina decided to open an antique and gift store as a tax write-off and, five years later, she was out of money and forced into bankruptcy. She returned to work baby-sitting and clerking at minimum wage. Her children abandoned her as Nina started to drink more. She substituted scotch for the prescribed medications she needed.

I loved Nina like family. I helped her with rent from time to time but, in the end, someone else loved her more. She found companionship at the rooming house where she lived, and I didn't see as much of her. She died of a stroke after falling out of the transvestite's bed. They had become the better friends, drinking buddies to be blunt, and they had been watching a movie and drinking at the time. They both liked scotch, and he'd had so much to drink he didn't even notice she had died until morning. Even so, her last hours on earth were spent with someone who gave her friendship and laughter.

Whether four-legged or two-legged, friends are loyal and helpful to the bitter end. The arrangement, of course, is reciprocal. To have a friend, you must first be a friend. There's no way of predicting who our dearest friends will be in life. Ideally, the man of our dreams will be that best friend forever and ever, but what if we find ourselves alone? After all these years, there's one thing I know for sure. Whether in times of loneliness, grief and boredom, or in periods of joy, someone seems to appear from out of nowhere just when a friend is needed most.

◆

MARGIE HARTFORD, author of *Sexual Savant at Sixty, Seventy, and Beyond* is a member of *The Writer's Circle* and published in *Interstices, the Orange County Anthology*. She started writing after she broke her foot in 1994. A friend gave her a dozen spiral notebooks and pens and told her to write.

Following Dave

In Rome, Dave ran out of pills.

"Gotta get more," he said, shaking the empty plastic tube.

A year ago Dave's shrink had put him on Tranxene to calm his anxiety. Dave was convinced he needed it to function.

I looked at Dave. He looked at me. He raised his arms and opened them, like he held an invisible beach ball.

We had to get more pills.

We left the hotel, trudged up the Aventine hill, a quiet residential part of Rome, away from traffic noise. On the Tiber side of the hill, we threaded through streets, crossed the Longotevere Aventino and increased speed on the flat beside the river. Just ahead I saw the island and its white medical buildings.

Dave used his self-taught Italian, which he studied at breakfast every morning while I read novels, to ask for a doctor. A young, white-coated man appeared. He and Dave fired rapid Italian at each other, the word "Tranxene" a major feature of their exchange.

The doctor wrote something on a piece of paper.

He pointed to the door and looked at his watch. "Pharmacy nearby, open another twenty minutes," I think he said.

Dave burst out the door. I followed.

He swept ahead, taking huge strides.

"Wait," I called.

"Come on." He looked at his watch. "They close in eighteen minutes."

"How far is it?"

"Four or five blocks, the doc said."

As the sun lowered in the cloud-wisped Roman sky, we sprinted across streets, up a hill, and around a corner. Dave had run out of pills. I puffed after him, feeling more and more foolish. Thirty-three years old, two children and an ex-husband at home, what was I doing running through the streets of Rome pursuing a man pursuing Tranxene?

I was humiliated for Dave, and for myself.

I continued to rush toward the Tranxene – following Dave, as I had followed him for the past two years, starting when he had wandered into the classroom that first evening and introduced himself as the teacher of the writing seminar that got me out of the house every week, to pursue my muse. Instead, I had pursued Dave.

The affair had been easy – he so handsome, I so needy – which explained the trip to Italy, the sprint across Rome.

The pharmacy was still open. Dave handed the pharmacist the piece of paper. In three minutes he had his pills. He put one in his mouth and swallowed.

In the street, Dave held out the tube. "You look like you could use one."

"No, thank you," I said.

The rest of the evening was uneventful. We ate at a tiny, cheap trattoria, walked back to the hotel, read, made love, slept.

Dave was still asleep when I eased out of bed, flicked on a dim light and packed my suitcase.

I didn't cry until the stewardess offered me coffee.

<hr/>

CAROL SANDERS lives in Coos Bay, OR, where she reads a lot, works on her novel and enjoys the rain and sun, sea and sky. Another story by this author appears in the Encore Section.

Martha Stothard

The Princess of Main Street

An icon
traveling between Chapman and La Veta,
she was the Princess of Main Street.
with an elegance about her
always the same clothes
but she seemed clean, pulled together.
She dragged her belongings in a luggage carrier,
neat and orderly.

My daughter tried to give her $20 once.
She refused.
She was not a panhandler,
never begged for anything.
It was a mystery how she survived.
She slept on a bench outside one of the shops
until they removed the bench.
Where she slept after that was a mystery.

She had been out there for close to two decades
and then one day
she was gone
but to where?
I want to know.
She was as much a fixture on Main Street
as the shops and fast food places,
CHOC and St. Joseph Hospitals,
traffic and ambulances,
but she was the Princess,
homeless,
but not a vagabond,
not an annoyance or in the way.

She was just the Princess of Main Street.
I miss her every single time I drive there.
I miss her. Does anyone else?

The Mending

Three yards of cloth
for a child's dress.
She watches mommy cut;
Mommy is expert at making things.
She is quick to pick it up,
her active mind not yet troubled
by the evil man next door.
She picks up a needle one day
and a little scrap of fabric.
The man next door has begun
to teach her to submit;
she is not the little inquisitive child
she was yesterday
but still the needle and the thread
can keep her occupied.
Her little soul has been ripped to shreds,
her talents grow each day.
All sorts of needles at her command
and the man next door persists
Five years have gone;
she is twelve years old,
a seamstress in the rough
But many more years will have to pass.
There is nothing her nimble fingers
cannot learn to do.
Then one day she picks up a pen,

pours out her heart on paper.
It is not a needle that repairs her soul
Ink on page starts the mending.

MARTHA STOTHARD has read her poetry at venues in Orange County, presenting her views on love, sex, body image, abuse, spiritual growth, and Wal-Mart. A sample of her work appeared in *Interstices: the Orange County Anthology.*

Nothing you write, if you hope to be any good, will ever come out as you first hoped.

– Lillian Helman

Song of Myself

Connor told me a joke: Why did the bee get married? He was seven. I tutored him in math. One day we were playing Battleship when he looked up at me over the wall of his board, his glasses slipping down his face, and whispered, "I can take my brain out of my head."

I blinked at him.

I laughed. I cried. Tears squeezed out the corners of my eyes. Little did Connor know that in a few days I would be having brain surgery for the second time. I was 26.

I learned about the different kinds of tears in the months before my second surgery. I cried when I was alone in my car, usually without prompting, as I zipped up and down the freeways. The tears swept across my entire being the way a rainfall sweeps across the desert in Southern California where I lived, briefly, leaving behind a feeling of appreciation for the warm, yellow sunshine. As the orange and fuchsia flames of the sunset lit up the sides of the mountains, I couldn't tell if my tears were of sadness, happiness, or relief. Often, I felt they were all three.

My second surgery was to reverse a procedure called Deep Brain Stimulation done three years earlier. During the procedure, the neurosurgeon implanted electrodes in my brain, connected by wires running down my neck to a pacemaker in my chest that interfered with abnormal electrical firing in my brain. It's the procedure that Michael J. Fox had done for his Parkinson's disease. I had a rare, related neuromuscular condition called dystonia. Or so my doctors thought.

After the Deep Brain Stimulation failed to relieve me of any of my symptoms, my neurologist and neurosurgeon believed that they might have misdiagnosed my dystonia. Or maybe the surgery just didn't work. Here's the thing about Deep Brain Stimulation: doctors don't understand *how* it works, only that it does, so when my surgery failed, no one could explain why.

I went to the mall. Under normal circumstances when I am not about to have my head cut open, I avoid the mall like swine flu. I don't do well with either crowds or the artificially-sweet scent of industrial-strength cleaners, but this time I was on a mission: to run up my credit card bill buying Victoria's Secret lingerie. After three years with a pacemaker the size of a tin of Altoids protruding from my chest, I was ready to be sexy again. I agonized over what color of nail polish to wear to my second surgery. The way I saw it, my nails would represent me as I lay on the cold slab of the operating table, half-naked and unconscious. In the end, I chose a pink named Tropical Fiesta for my fingernails and Citron Green for my toes.

When my kids at the tutoring center where I worked asked me about the 2-inch scar on my chest, I made up stories. "Mauled by a tiger," I said to one. To another, I said, "Bit by a dolphin." And my favorite: "Attacked by a hummingbird." Finally, Katrina, age 11, got mad and demanded of me, "Didn't anyone ever teach you that it's wrong to tell lies?"

It helped to be secretly in love with my neurosurgeon, who practiced yoga and wore rock-climbing shoes and bowties. Doesn't everyone fall in love with his or her surgeons, even just a little bit? My neurosurgeon had touched my brain. He was the only man in my life up until this point who had tried to figure out how my head worked. *Sighhhhh*. He did it with a handsaw. I asked my Dad how it was done only after it was all over. I hadn't wanted to know beforehand. I wondered, *how wide is the skull?* How many inches separate the inside of my head from the rest of the world?

Before the first surgery, I watched a PBS documentary about Deep Brain Stimulation. I saw people with much worse dystonias than mine, people who couldn't talk due to tongue and jaw spasms, people whose necks twisted and stuck to their shoulders, people whose limbs shook, people bent at the waist, unable to walk. When they turned on their pacemakers, presto! They were magically freed of contortions. They stood up straight and still. The actor Lamar Burton, the guy with the funny silver glasses from "Star Trek," introduced the documentary. Standing before a deep blue velvet backdrop, he intoned, "The people you are about to witness can be called cyborgs."

I threw a shoe at Lamar Burton. "We're not cyborgs!" I yelled, "We're just people who want to be normal!"

I had to wake up during the first surgery while the surgeons were placing the electrodes in my brain. They needed to hear my brain activity on the EEG machine. They orchestrated the surgery in intervals, first the electrodes, then the wire, then the pacemaker. In total, it took six hours. They woke me after three. Warm white blankets swaddled me, and pressure cuffs tightened on my legs, moving the blood up and down. A plastic halo, screwed on at my temples, kept my head from moving. The brain has no pain receptors. Except for the tightness of the halo and a pressure at the top of my head, I felt nothing at all. I could hear the EEG machine. My brain sounded like the static in between radio stations. It snapped, crackled and popped like breakfast cereal. It sounded like deep space.

On the sun, electricity shoots across the surface to create bright orange flames. My brain was the sun, and the doctors, nurses, and anesthesiologist were orbiting around me. I lay there trying to make sense of the sounds I heard. *Were they a code? Did they sound like a song?* And then I sunk back into sleep.

The neurosurgeon bored tracks into my brain, threaded wires inside of me, and slipped the pacemaker into my flesh through the bleeding slit in my skin that, when mended, would become my scar, and then he undid it. The wires traveled backwards up my neck, red and blue like my veins.

So much in this world is a mystery. Tunnel a wormhole to the center of the mind, and you can be made better, happier, free. Or maybe you won't be granted what you wish for. Who's to say if you have been changed?

When I was healing from the second surgery, I didn't have much pain, just exhaustion. I'd wake up, go to the kitchen, fix myself food, eat, nap for four hours, and repeat. For days, I didn't have enough energy to watch television. Mostly, I lay in bed on Vicodin and watched the sun travel up and down the wall of my bedroom.

I thought of the female writer I'd read about whose doctors cancelled her lobotomy when she won a major literary prize. Lamar, I was only a cyborg temporarily. In the end, after the ball with the glass slipper, I turned back into a human. Poof!

After I recovered, I put a new CD in my car on the freeway. An exuberant, childlike voice reassured me that *it was okay if I didn't know how to put my heart back together; it was okay if it all sounded like science fiction, and it was just my life.*

The name of the song was "Self."

I went back to work wearing headbands and scarves to cover the top of my head. I gave thanks for the kids I taught, who explained the world to me.

Before my second surgery, Connor had told me about the bee getting married, and I'd forgotten the punch line before I even got home.

Afterwards, I knew I was different in a way I couldn't explain, different from before.

Like that, summer was over. Wireless, we moved forward into fall.

———◆———

MOIRA WILLIAMS, a former intern at McSweeney's Publishing in San Francisco, is currently working as a tutor in Spanish and French. She edited *The Re-View,* a feminist journal, while at Scripps College in Claremont. She is the 2010 recipient of the *Mona Schreiber Prize for Humorous Fiction.*

Simon Says

King Simon sat on his throne and sighed. His guards stood like statues, awaiting their orders. He sighed again, this time louder. There was still no response.

"Well, go ahead," he snapped. "Ask me what's wrong!"

"Sir," said one of the guards timidly, "is that a direct order?"

Simon grunted irritably. "Yes! Simon says ask me what's the matter!"

The guards all said, in a perfectly-timed chorus, "What's the matter, King Simon?"

"I'm fed up with this! No one takes initiative anymore! They just do whatever I tell them to do without a single thought in their heads."

There was no answer.

"Simon says respond!"

"Well, King Simon, you decreed that nothing could be done without your OK. Or else…(the man swallowed)…or else he is banished to the kingdom of Out."

Simon felt rather than heard a fearful inhalation from each guard. Nobody wanted to live in Out. It was desolate and lonely, and one's only companions were other criminals of the state, those who had refused to obey Simon or misunderstood what was an order and what was not an order.

"If we want to remain in the fair kingdom of In, we must obey His Majesty, King Simon."

"All hail King Simon!" they shouted as a chorus.

"I am going to take a walk," King Simon said after a time.

Without thinking, one of the guards retrieved his coat and handed it to the despot. Simon looked at the young man, fuming.

"What have you done, you fool?"

Realizing his error, the guard kneeled. "Please Your Majesty. Have mercy. I knew that in a moment you were going to ask for your coat! I merely anticipated."

"You are banished!" The other guards cried in unison. "To Out with you!"

The guard hung his head and left the court.

"Alas," sighed King Simon. "He was a fine guard. But it had to be done." He rose from his throne.

"Simon says walk." The king and his guards wandered the fair kingdom. A few minutes later, one of the guards noticed that the king was growing tired.

"Stop!" he cried. A few of the guards stopped immediately.

There was a silence. "King Simon didn't say to stop!" the king roared, outraged.

Four guards walked, heads down, toward the kingdom of Out.

Simon looked around him. There were only two obedient guards left, walking in place so as not to disobey the king's orders.

"You have done well my sons," King Simon acknowledged gratefully. "Come and receive your prize."

The more ambitious of the two guards walked eagerly forward, awaiting his rich reward. But alas!

"*Simon* didn't say," the king cried. "From henceforth, thou art banished!"

And away he walked, to join the others in the kingdom of Out.

And now there was but one guard who awaited him, standing proudly at attention. And King Simon sighed, nodded, removed his crown, and said, "Sir Kevin, I name you my successor, King of In."

The guard proudly donned the throne. "You are Simon II," the former-king acknowledged.

"Regroup everyone!" called the new king. "Simon says regroup! Simon grants full amnesty to all those who disobeyed, provided they agree to obey the new administration of King Simon II."

And yet, nobody returned. Confused, Simon I and Simon II trekked to Out to see what was the matter.

"We are happy here," said one of the guards in reply to Simon's question. "Here there is the possibility to rise in the world. I myself have gone from commoner to knight to prince. Soon, I shall be king of the fair kingdom of Four Square."

"Here," a girl explained, "you are rewarded for your actions rather than chided for your mistakes. If you win a duel with a nobleman, you gain a higher status. In your kingdom, Your Majesty, there is only obedience and disobedience."

"We no longer wish to obey you," said the guard who had accidentally given Simon I his coat. "We prefer to make our own decisions."

"But Simon says return!" cried Simon II. "Simon *says!*"

The citizens of Four Square eyed the young figure in king's clothing. Then, a resident who had never lived in In asked a very simple question, "Who's Simon?"

SARA BALMUTH is an archaeology student at the University of California, San Diego. She is the author of a variety of unpublished short stories and a single novella. She writes, plays the violin, and reads when she is not studying for finals.

Each book is, in a sense, an argument with myself, and I would write it, whether it is ever published or not.

—Patricia Highsmith

PAT JACKSON-COLANDO

Visit Grandma Minnie

Some people see things. Some hear voices. Others have no imagination whatsoever. They leave all imagination to God, then they don't even live in the present to appreciate His best creations: their own selves on Mama Earth, who's resplendent even in my unsightly yard.

I mostly stay inside, away from my bramble bushes and slovenly grass. I do stray up the pebble path to the mailbox to pick up my daily junk mail after I see Amos, the postman, amble by. I love being nestled in my home as I peek at Earth through parted lace curtains. I feel safe, swathed in a reality that is entitled to hopes and lies and dreams.

I have forgotten the past. It would be a waste of space in a mind that can predict the future. And the present isn't too comfortable because I have arthritis in my knees. I am Grandma Minnie and people pay me big money for what I see and hear and portend – even pretend at times - for their future. It's a gift. And it buys a lot of Advil and weed.

A long black limousine just glided alongside the fence of my yard a minute ago and stopped abreast of the wretched hanging gate. I could afford a new gate, but the look is atmospheric. A hunched gentleman in a coat, cap, and shoes, all nearly the same hue as his dark night skin, emerged, walking stately as any man can. He looked around lightly to take in the details of my entire swatch of landscape before he opened the limo's back door. His guardedness was second nature, gained from careful training or dreadful circumstance. I longed to see his future, but I knew that he was not here for his own reasons, so I saved my practical energy. It was Wednesday afternoon and I had already done a week of work for a woman of my avocation.

The tall man who unfolded from the limousine was dressed less impeccably. His blue jeans may have been expensive, but they were shredded and patched in intriguing detail. His open white shirt had red stars woven among blue stripes inside its collar and cuffs that took the eye away from his hairless chest.

His swagger was easy as he climbed my sturdy steps.

"I've been expecting you," I say, smiling.

This knocks his swagger askew and stops the words he'd planned, leaving them hanging in midair like his left foot. Visibly puzzled, he nervously runs manicured fingers through his longish hair.

"Please come inside. Would you like tea or bourbon?"

This eases his nervousness and his teeth gleam through the smile of thick lips. "Bourbon. Are you Grandma Minnie?"

When I nod, he turns to signal the black man, who drives over to the pebbled space under the hickory tree's heavy branches. He'll be cool in the shade while he waits on this man's business. It'd gotten a little steamy out here in the country, more than we are used to back in these hills.

"I almost feel like I don't have to tell you why I'm here, such is your reputation, Grandma Minnie. My friend Charlie said you even helped him win a half-million bucks! Was that his luck or yours when you predicted the outcome of those horse races last month?"

"Now, Mr. Evans. You can't expect me to divulge the business of another of my clients or the methods of my talents," I teased him mildly. "You've come a long way to see me. Why don't you tell me what you want of me?" I favored being direct. It took me longer than I liked to admit to predict an unknown's future. I had data and impressions to collect, collate, and consider. I lumbered down into my rocker, my ma's gift to me, with wood that never creaked like my knees. "You know my fees, I assume, and you are prepared to pay, in cash, no matter what the consequences. No matter what happens when the future becomes the present and then shifts into the past?"

"Yes, Ma-am. Mind if I sit?"

Mr. Evans seated himself gingerly on the faded plaid sofa, almost as if he expected split ketchup packets to squirt out from the cushions. I re-focused on the expensively tattered blue jeans and, as the pant legs hiked, I noted gaudy boots of alligator leather embedded with other animal skins up-and-down the sides. The heels were what had made him seem tall, I noted with amusement. I handed him bourbon that I'd poured into a sliver of a glass, placing a pitcher of water and a larger glass by its side. Back in my sweet little kitchen, decorated with hearts and voodoo signs, I heaped my glass with ice and poured myself some tea. I brought an ice bucket with me and set it on the coffee table between us.

He fumbled with preparation of just the right drink, visibly changing his mind between ice, or not, several times. At last the drink was prepared and he gulped the contents clean.

"Well, Grandma." He'd already become familiar, dropping my surname with that bourbon gulp, "I need your help. Well, you know that and, well, this is awkward for me. My attorney has strongly advised me to not come to see you and my wife would have a hissey-fit dance on my head if she knew. She's temperamental. This topic has made her testy, but I ventured anyway. My driver, Jerome, says you're talented and true."

"Thank you, Mr. Evans," I stated simply. I remained silent. It wasn't my turn to talk.

When I didn't speak more or offer him more to drink, Mr. Evans knew that it was time to speak his needs and he began the way they always do, by asking me to call him by his first name.

"Elvis, it is," I smiled pleasantly. He was beginning to settle in; there'd been no ketchup geyser and the couch had not sprung a coil from under its slumpy cushions. He was going to be all right.

"I'm having a time," he tried. My silence forced him to proceed. "I have a business manager who pays for everything in my life - and even a few things in other people's lives, now that I have an ex-wife as well as a wife."

I kept smiling, noticing that he was cycling more quickly toward his purpose than I'd expected. It must have been that he knew that my time was his money.

"I think that he, well, my manager, Carl, gave my Cayman banking information to the damn government and I want to know what's going to happen. I mean do I have time to make my way out of this and, well, what's going to happen next and when? What can I do to stop a catastrophe?" His forehead was alternately creasing and expanding, a mirror of how his mind was working.

Instantly the numbers of two accounts flashed in neon in my mind. "Excuse me, Elvis, I think that my tea has already run through me." And, as I turned the corner into the hallway, I swiftly entered my room and wrote those numbers on my bedside tablet. The use of the bathroom had been a ruse, but I flushed the toilet anyway and washed my hands slowly, lovingly. The symbolism of this act was not lost in my musings and I smiled at myself in the oval mirror of the medicine chest. "I love you, Grandma Minnie's mind," I intoned. It's in these moments that I feel closest to God: His gifts, His glory.

A few moments later, back to rocking in Ma's chair, I smiled so that my client would continue to tell me his business and his concerns, knowing that soon enough he would learn that Grandma Minnie had solved his problem. With a few computer keystrokes from my gifted grandson's hands, there would be no more bank accounts in the Caymans and he would be blameless with the Feds. I wasn't going to worry about the wife and ex-wife. Simmering sexpots would grow claws, but Grandma would be having knee replacement and some plastic surgery soon, perhaps in Costa Rica under a whole new name.

I hear that lace is fashionable in the tropics, so the lace curtains may embrace the shoulders below my smooth face and neck, flirting with knees that are dancing. My grandchildren do love to dance!

———◆———

PAT JACKSON-COLANDO, a licensed speech-language pathologist and public speaker, has written articles for newspapers, magazines, periodicals, and grants for nonprofits. She has received numerous awards for community service and enjoys writing while her husband watches sports.

SUZANNE PATTERSON

Riding the Red Trolley

The sight of the red trolley (blue line) approaching as I descend the steps of the 709 is always a happy one for me. It lightens my load to one of anticipation and cheerfulness. Looking back and calling "thank you" to the bus driver I see almost daily, I throw my backpack over one shoulder and begin jogging toward the station. I love seeing the Mexicans standing near the station with a cup of coffee in one hand and a plate of rolled tacos or tamales in the other, chatting in Español to one another. Carlos at the Woody's Lunch Wagon is always there and greets everybody, "Buenos dias!" and "gracias," with a friendly smile. Plus, coffee is only a dollar.

Perhaps it would not be so charming if I had not recently lived and worked in Mexico City for a year and a half and ridden the trolley bus and underground metro daily to the various business districts around the city. I loved the physical and emotional contact of so many people squeezed against one another, especially first thing in the morning. The Mexicans are very clean people and, unlike people on public transportation in the US, smell aqua fresh and sweet. They don't expose other passengers to any gurgling throat-clearing sounds or open displays of whatever they're eating.

I have always been a "change addict" as one perceptive job coach once told me, and now every day is an opportunity to enjoy that addiction since I live in Chula Vista, South San Diego. I returned to California at age 58 in 2009 in the middle of a really terrible recession. I sought work as an ESL teacher here; there are about 17 language schools in San Diego, more than in any other city in the US, outside of New York and Miami. Because it's a border city, I figured I'd find work on one side of the border or the other.

Although I had savings when I arrived, I was not prepared for eight months of almost no employment except for temporary positions of about three weeks each every couple of months. And to add to my dilemma, since I had been working out of the country for a year and a half, I did not qualify for unemployment.

I threw out my lifeline, substitute teaching, first in July to the districts in north San Diego where I had rented an apartment with my son, and then to Chula Vista and National City in the South, where I moved to live with my Mexican amiga. By February, 2010, I was up and running with almost daily jobs from the two elementary school districts in Chula Vista and National City. I was bilingual, trained as a special education teacher and could teach all of the grades, thereby filling any vacant position. And the kids loved me. I taught them art.

Riding the trolley lines to National City, downtown, Mission Valley, and South Chula Vista regularly was an opportunity to take the pulse of the nation. What one learns about on the trolleys are the communities of sub-cultures surviving in the undercurrents of San Diego's business economy. One meets the Mexican children and workers traveling from Tijuana to San Diego daily for school and work, leaving Tijuana at 4:30 in the morning to cross the "line." And there are the homeless white and black Americans, women and men, and the many new immigrants from Central Africa, Iraq, Syria, Vietnam and Burma. They come in droves and are taken care of by the Relocation Center in University Heights, the largest center in the country, since San Diego is the first port of entry in the US for refugees coming from all over the world.

There are many moments of experiencing simple humanity on the trolley. I have seen homeless people greet each other by name and share a breakfast or ask about the other's health. I have seen two men who came out of the same prison embrace each other. Some of the homeless citizens I have spoken with have worked all of their lives and have nothing to show for it. Many receive services in this county. We have one of the highest populations of veterans and many of the returning veterans have become homeless. One military base set up a tent city for homeless veterans.

One day there was a fight on the trolley. A drunken man dropped his bicycle on a homeless man in the space between cars. "You're not supposed to have your bike here." The red-headed drunk became livid, his face the color of his hair, and he threw a punch. The fight began; the drunk was knocked to the floor. Suddenly, a petite, older Mexican woman got up from her seat and broke up the fight by standing between the two men. She simply grabbed onto the back of the drunken man's shirt and held on. When the security guard entered the car, she defended her captive even though he wasn't supposed to have his bicycle between the trolley cars.

I love talking with some of the older people I have met on the trolley. I met Jose at the Breyer Trolley station. He was a 72-year-old Mexican man standing next to an old bicycle with a flat tire as he talked animatedly on a cell phone. When he finished speaking, I said to him, "Your tire is flat."

"I know," he said, and he gave me a long explanation about buying an expensive tire tube that had failed. He said he was going to buy a new tire soon. "Change," he said. "Things are continually changing." He pointed to the newspaper stand, "Like the Union Tribune. Been reading it for 40 years and now it's got a new logo. A big company back east bought it and had to change the look." He pointed to the modern archetype letters U T on a diagonal across the top left corner of the paper.

Then he motioned to a young adolescent with a spiky red Mohawk. The boy stood on the other side of the tracks smoking a cigarette. "Things are always changing, so that no one knows what's real anymore, like him listening to his iPod and playing video games."

The elderly gent moved on to the latest hot topic – immigration. "I think people shouldn't protest immigration laws. We need to be able to enforce them and get rid of the bad element. I'm not a racist, don't get me wrong, but I've been an American for 40 years, fought for my country and paid taxes. People shouldn't be coming over here, thinking they can stay for free, and then cause trouble."

When the trolley pulled up beside us, he said, "Know that I love you." He smiled a toothless smile and walked off, dragging his bicycle.

I considered, briefly, meeting a romantic liaison on the rails, but the last one, although a little handsome, was eating a piece of barbecued chicken out of a crumpled paper bag when he walked up to start a conversation as I waited for the trolley. He was immediately disqualified, in spite of maintaining a fairly intelligent conversation.

The trolleys keep running. The first language on the blue line, Old Town, San Ysidro/Tijuana, continues to be Spanish, and the mood of this microcosm of the nation is optimistic. Perhaps it is the beautiful sunshine and semi-tropical environment of San Diego that keeps us warm and happy. Or the predominance of the Mexican people, the third happiest people in the world. Or the way the trolley winds past the Navy ports, the Santa Fe Depot, the harbor of San Diego, Fashion Valley, San Diego State University and all the way to the town of Santee. Whatever it is, the red car keeps me going and feeling that life is worth living. I gently release the illusive future, freeing the doubt and uncertainty into the air, and sigh a deep sigh of relief.

SUZANNE PATTERSON is a professional technical writer/trainer and ESL/bi-lingual teacher residing in Chula Vista, CA. She writes a column "Cultural Contrasts" for the *Enterprise*, an online newspaper. She has a writing and translation business in Mexico City and is in the process of moving this company to the border cities. Her hobbies are painting, drawing, and writing creatively.

Noosha Ravaghi

My Loving Mother

I was born on the second day of October in 1970. Apparently, that was also the day my mother got amnesia and, eventually, used her imagination and creativity to fabricate new facts.

My loving mother, who had gotten pregnant before getting married and wanted to cover it up, suddenly forgot my birthday in October, and decided, based on her calculations, that March 30th was a more appropriate day for my birth. Even her friends who had been at the hospital the day I was born also conveniently forgot my birthday and sent me birthday wishes in March.

It didn't stop there, though. My mother got a second birth certificate from the hospital with the appropriate date. Don't you love the power of having connections? That's right. I was born twice, once on October 2nd, 1970, and once on March 30th, 1971; and I have hospital records to prove it. Seriously, how many people in the world can prove, with documentation, that they have been born twice?

Although my official identification papers reflect my fake birthday, all my close friends and all my relatives on my father's side have always celebrated my birthday on October 2nd. In my loving mother's family, it's a completely different story. That, however, doesn't matter much because shortly after I was born – one of the two times – my loving mother decided that she didn't want a child in the first place and left us, so I grew up with my father, my paternal grandparents – may they both rest in peace – and all the secretaries in the Persian Literature departments of all the universities in which my father taught.

The memories I have from my childhood mostly involve a desk in a classroom close to my father's classroom because I remember always hearing his voice loudly reading Ferdowsi's Book of Kings. The department secretaries changed from university to university, and the language they spoke changed from country to country. Yes, there was a lot of change in my life during my childhood, and I was good at adapting to new cultures and languages.

The only constant in my life has been my loving mother's birthday cards. After forty years, I still receive a greeting card, on March 30th every year, signed "Your Loving Mother" and wishing me a happy birthday. I have to admit that I admire her persistence in holding on to her fabricated truths. I once wrote to her, "Give it up. Who cares if you got pregnant before you got married? It's not like you were a teenager when you got pregnant; you were twenty-seven years old. Everyone around you knows the truth anyway, so why don't you just let it go? Have a little respect for the life you brought into this world. No? Fine. Have a little respect for yourself!" I don't know what I was thinking when I wrote that. The only response I got to that was, "My Dear Daughter, you sent me a letter that makes absolutely no sense to me. Are you sure you addressed it correctly?" It felt like Robert De Niro was saying, "Are you talking to me?"

Unfortunately, the fake-birthday cards I receive at my post office box every year are not the only way I "hear" from this stubborn stranger who calls herself my loving mother. I could write a whole book on the advantages and disadvantages of technology, with a highlighted focus on the latter. Technology has allowed my loving mother to introduce her monologues in different ways. From voicemail to email, her messages always come in a series and they all say basically the same thing, that I'm not a good daughter, that she is the best mother anyone could wish for, and that anyone who says otherwise has been hired by my father to tell such lies only to destroy her reputation.

One evening after work, I looked at my cell phone to see if I had any messages and I was surprised to see I had eighteen missed calls and six voicemail messages, all from my loving mother. I listened to my messages one after another. Now, you may think that I'm making this up, but I'm not. I have not one, but two witnesses. I met two of my friends that night for dinner and let both of them listen to all my messages from that day. While one of them knew my loving mother and expected nothing less from her, the other one was so surprised that she dislocated her jaw from opening her mouth so much in disbelief.

2:13pm – Hello, N… This is your loving mother. I miss you and I can't wait another day to see you. Call me immediately.

2:42pm – Hello, N… I called you earlier and left a message for you, but I think it didn't go through because you haven't called me back. I miss you. Call me as soon as you get this message.

3:01pm – Hello! I called you and left you several messages. I don't understand why you haven't returned my calls. I'm waiting!

3:50pm – This is your mother. I'm just worried about you and I need to hear your voice to know that you are ok. Please call me back.

4:18pm – My heart is not beating right. I think I'll have to call 911. If you call and I don't answer, please check the hospital.

4:56pm – Never mind! My printer is fixed. I don't need to see you after all!

Fortunately, the same technology also allows me to delete these messages. However, from time to time, when I have a few extra minutes in my day and I'm in the mood for a little fun, I listen to or read these messages instead of deleting them and wonder how someone with such great talent has not become famous. What a waste! Her stories are more interesting than many published novels I've read, and they reflect an amazing imagination.

September 14, 2005 – 6:25am

Dear N…

I haven't seen you in a long time. You're my only daughter, and my only wish is to see you. Please call me as soon as possible so we can arrange to meet. I miss you terribly!

I love you.

Your Loving Mother

September 14, 2005 – 6:45am

Dear N…

I don't blame you for not responding to the email that I sent you half an hour ago. You are not a mother yet. That's why you can't imagine how much I love you. If you knew how much I loved you, you would come and visit me very often. I took care of you and carried you around for nine months until you were born. Now that I'm getting older, it's your duty to come and take care of me.

I love you.

Your Loving Mother

September 14, 2005 – 7:33am

Dear N…

How many mothers do you think you have?

The most important person in each person's life is their mother.

I don't know what your father has taught you, but if he had educated you well enough, you would have learned to reply to your mother's messages. He has filled your head with lies. Anyway, this is the third email I've sent in the last two hours and I have not received any reply from you.

I'm your mother, and you need to call me!

Your Loving Mother

September 14, 2005 – 8:07am

Dear N…

I'm very disappointed! You leave me no alternative but to contact the police and tell them that you are trying to kill me. That's right. I'm a worrying person and the stress of not hearing from you could kill me. You are a murderer, and I know your father has hired you to do what he couldn't finish 35 years ago. Your father has always been jealous of your love for me and has brainwashed you. I will have both of you arrested, even if it's the last thing I do!

Your Loving Mother

———

NOOSHA RAVAGHI, born in Iran in 1970, spent most of her life traveling around the world. She now lives in Aliso Viejo, California, where she has been editing books and teaching English and French to children as well as adults since 1997.

When the writing starts, listen.

— Marianne Moore

Diana Pardee

Ode to Billy Collins

It was one of those Barnes & Noble nights
of my recently renewed subscription to singleness.
Too early to go home to my tidy solitude,
too late to go anywhere else besides my local pub,
where men in sweaty t-shirts trolling with free drink lures
demonstrate only occasional elegance of intellect.

Bored and irritated with politics,
I found another literary novel to add
to my collection of defenses against
spontaneous, meaningless sex,
then headed to Poetry, recalling
a certain irritating label
of Maya Angelou as a hack
writing in tiresome clichés,
which I felt compelled to disprove.

He caught my eye as I browsed the shelves,
the word "sailing" emblazoned on his back.
With a whimsical tale of three blind mice
and how did they find each other, anyway,
I was hooked like a Bonita with a barb in my gills,
soaring out of the depths in a wide arc
to land with a splat on the transom
filleted on the spot.

Here was a man with the heart of a poet,
eyes punctuated with curving ellipses that told of
decades of laughter, squinting into the sun.

If my heart weren't already in the bait bucket,
it would have been exposed and arrhythmic.

Unwilling to appear too desperate
I wandered to a chair with Maya,
who convinced me she couldn't hold my interest
after only three clichés.
When he joined me there,
she was entirely forgotten.
Committing to a shared latte,
he revealed himself as a man who would
scan a rollercoaster with a pragmatic eye
to determine it's worthiness,
then ride with exuberance
as if it were the first time
every time.

At this point there was no doubt
he was coming home with me.
Even though my self-imposed contract clearly stated
NO MEN for 6 months, this was
synchronicity at its most devious.
After the initial filleting,
I had no backbone,
nor recollection of the need to have one.

Without revealing intimate details
I can tell you that between the sheets,
lying by the fire or sampling impromptu interludes
on the kitchen table, if this man were a recipe
he would be a handmade pasta al dente
drenched in a secret family sauce with
complex overtones of chilies and goat cheese,
amid subtle undertones of clove and anis

that seems at the moment of touching your tongue,
even better than sex, kama sutra, tantric or otherwise.
Needless to say, this one is a keeper.
I only wish I had bought the hardbound version.

The Blues

Play that Blues, Love

Bathe me in bass

Pluck at my core

That tantalizing lamentation

Leaves me dripping

No honey dreams here

But a smoky, sultry flow

Percolates through me

Sap slicks my thighs

Probing rhythms

Yield to ancient pulsing

That reminds me

Why I love the Blues.

Cello Master

They are one.
This master breathes life
Into her cello curves
Embracing her
He strokes, coaxes
Swaying in search
Of her soul notes
In a melancholy
Minor key.

He drifts back to me
Floating in liquid vibrations
Deft hands stroke
My neck
His bow probes
My core
Thighs wrap me
In musk scented skin
Mold to me
Become me
Honeyed sounds turn
To steam in my gut
Bees swarm
In quivering spirals
That race through
My veins.

We are one.
This master breathes life
Into my cells
Vivid past resurfaces
On a sweet swell of life
Each note lingers

Foretelling endings
Briny tears
One long last note
Of liquid caress
Leaves me again
Drowning in silence.

DIANA PARDEE has participated in a number of poetry and fiction groups for the past ten years. A resident of Laguna Niguel, she's currently a member of the South Orange County Critique group and part of a journaling workshop in Aliso Viejo.

We don't see things as they are, we see them as we are."

— Anais Nin

KATHY AKAGHA

Letter from the Third Musketeer

I heard it again today – that I'm lucky. I've heard this for the last twenty-four years. Since the age of eight, I was told I was lucky. Everyone said it. I don't think I fully understood what this meant back then. I wondered what my parents would say about it – if they were still alive. But they're not alive because when I was eight my entire family was killed in a plane crash on our way to a Kenyan safari. My older sister and brother, Aaliyah and Ali, also died. They were twins. They were so much fun to be around – we were the three musketeers and they used to treat me like I was their triplet even though they were five years older. Now they're long gone and left me solo. My whole family ceased to exist, perished – over lions and tigers and bears – oh why?

I was indeed the sole survivor of the accident and escaped with minor scratches, but I've always seen my "lucky" situation differently.

I had an extended family, Uncle Willie and his brood, who took me in when my own became one with the earth. My uncle, Willie, was a jolly, six-foot-five, giant, who had gray hairs coming out of every opening and seemed to have a uni-brow of gray above his eyes. He was my father's much older only sibling. Sadly, he'd experienced loss five years before my arrival when his wife died from a sudden heart attack. His children, my cousins, were all in their early and late twenties when I entered their lives. They wanted nothing to do with me and were not afraid to say so.

I followed Cousin Jena around the house like an afternoon shadow, a mini version of her. She used to scream at me, "WHY ARE YOU ALWAYS ON MY SIX?" She was twenty-three and in the Marine Corps then. I just wanted so much for her to understand that I was eight, not six, but of course, she didn't mean my age. She disliked that I was always following her around, so she meant that I should get off her back and do my own thing.

117

Jena's 27-year-old brother, Dwayne, had no use for me either. At that time, he had no use for anyone except his drug-dealer. I heard he made room for a mistress named "Crystal," whose last name was shortened to "Meth" when she arrived on the streets.

There was also 21-year-old Cousin Steve. I called him Creepy Sieve because he had zits the size and spacing of holes in a sieve. The holes separated good from evil. As a kid, I believed the evil stayed on his face and the good jumped deck to get the fuck away from him. Creepy Sieve wasn't all there in the noggin either. He was expelled from high school for pushing a girl into an empty janitor's closet where he tried to grab and suck on her titties. He admitted that he had a cow fetish and when he bum-rushed her and forced her into the closet he said, "Com'ere, cow." She kicked him where it counted and ran as fast as she could to the principal's office. She eventually escaped to the grassy fields of Northern California where she lives with her "kids" – she raises goats for a living.

So, I was the youngest, not only in my immediate family but in the entire Johnston clan. No one could really relate to me, and I could relate to no one. So that is how I learned to live life, un–relatable. I needed no one. I often wondered, *Why me?* Why were Mom, Dad, Aaliyah, and Ali chosen to experience life-after-death? Why was I left behind – alone even when surrounded by people? But people only knew me from the outside and by what I let them see. No one knew the extent of me, Serena Johnston, or that I was screaming inside for someone to really hear me. I'm still waiting today. Good night world. Truly unlucky.

KATHY AKAGHA, a resident of Lake Forest, enjoys writing fiction and poetry and participates in *Saturday Mornings Coffee & Critique*. The above is excerpted from a longer work titled *SBC*.

My First Kiss

"I have to get back. I have a lot of homework." The movie was over and I was ready to go home. So why were we still sitting in Rick's car?

"I'd really like to kiss you," he said.

"If I don't get home soon, I'm going to be up all night." I tried to sound urgent. "I have an English paper due tomorrow."

Rick adjusted the rear-view mirror, examined his freckled chin, and patted his wiry hair. Then he turned towards me and said, "Just one kiss."

I didn't know Rick that well and now I was letting him reach over and touch my hair. At sixteen, I hadn't been on very many dates so I was kind of curious. "Sure, okay, you can kiss me."

Rick leaned over the gearshift and touched his lips to mine. He brushed them gently over my cheek and I felt their warmth. All of a sudden, I wasn't in a hurry to get home and do my homework. The street lamp flickered, a car engine revved, and people walked by.

When Rick put his key in the ignition and started the car, it was too soon. "I gotta get going," he said. "I told you I wait tables at Roberto's Steak House. I get real good tips on Thursdays." He spoke as if nothing had happened.

The next morning I got to school early and ran into him in the hallway. Thankfully, there weren't too many people around. I gave him a smile that said, "We made out last night in your car, and it was amazing."

Rick looked at me and narrowed his eyes. Then he pivoted and took off in the opposite direction. I followed him. "Rick it's me." He sped up, sliding on the waxed linoleum floor before bolting out the entryway.

That's when I finally got it; I wouldn't be going on a second date with Rick.

You might say my date ended badly, but I don't see it that way. After all, Rick gave me my first real kiss. I don't remember the movie, and I can't recall too much about Rick, but I'll always remember that first kiss.

MELISSA SOKOL, an elementary school teacher, is published in *Interstices, the Orange County Anthology*. She participates in *Saturday Mornings Coffee & Critique* where she is completing a children's chapter book titled *Clarissa's Crows*.

JULIE CRANDALL

The Crusty Old German Teacher

I like "nice." I like the smiles and friendliness that come with it. I like the southern hospitality variety. I even like the type that is sticky sweet. But what I learned from my high school German teacher is that I'll take "good" over "nice" any day.

Frau Hodgera was the meanest teacher in the school and we all knew it. She sat perched on her stool behind the podium, red pen in hand, grade book spread out, scowling at the wretched student who was ill prepared for class or who happened to mispronounce the proper German dialect. Every student at Glendora High School knew she was mean as a snake, and I personally can attest to the stomachache I'd have everyday before entering that classroom. But even so, every once in awhile, I'd wonder what was behind that icy cold façade. So when our social studies teacher gave us the assignment to interview someone who had lived through WWII, I thought of Frau Hodgera.

I was nervous when we sat down for that interview. I'll never forget how I got the tape recorder out only to have her tell me in a quiet menacing way, "no tape recorder." I remember the way her eyes met mine as if to ask, 'do you really care about what I have to tell you?' I did… and pretty soon the assignment didn't matter; the interview didn't matter. The only thing that did matter was this woman who sat in front of me, and the stories that have never left me.

When Frau Hodgera was a young woman – maybe 19 or 20 – she was still living in Germany. She watched Hitler take power and she watched as nationalism swept the country, along with a tide of hatred for anyone who was different. People – friends and neighbors – started disappearing. The main target for the fear and hate were the Jews, of course. She had a choice, to be paralyzed with fear or to act in defiance of the evil she was witnessing. So this young woman began to hide these Jewish people – first friends, then strangers. It was dangerous. If she had been caught it would have meant certain death for her and her family. She told me there are some things worth risking your life for.

I never looked at Frau Hodgera the same after that. No, she never eased up, she never softened, she never had an especially nice word for me, but in her life story I saw what it meant to be "good." In the hallways of my high school, I saw plenty of people who were "nice," but how many would have chosen "goodness" if they'd been in her place. I never confused "nice" and "good" again.

When parents are asked what they want for their children, they tend to say that they want their children to be "nice" or they want their children to be "happy." Perhaps our priority should be shaping our children toward goodness. We do this by taking "goodness" seriously. We live in a world where genocide and "ethnic cleansing" are realities, where people fight, hate, and kill because of their differences. We hope our children will never have to risk their lives to save another person like Frau Hodgera did, but if "goodness" means anything then we must lead our children toward the courage that it sometimes takes.

Striving for "goodness" must have some real meaning in our everyday lives. Thinking about others, doing for others, reaching across barriers, standing up for someone who can't stand up for himself, recognizing the real or potential good in others – it's what we are called to do every day. It's downright counter cultural in a world that whispers to us – and our kids – a thousand messages a day of 'it's all about you; feel good; consume; you deserve it; treat yourself; find your bliss.'

"Nice" will always make my day; I'm crazy about it. It makes me feel good. But what moves and inspires me more are the things of goodness – love, altruism, sacrifice, and compassion…. the values of the Christian… the secular humanist… the Muslim… the Jew… the atheist…. values that might just bring all of us together.

My crusty old German teacher with her sour look and red pen wasn't nice, but she had the courage to take goodness seriously and changed the lives of others, including mine.

◆

JULIE CRANDALL is a preschool teacher who lives in Mooresville, NC. A mother of two, she writes on parenting and contributes regularly to *Tapestry*, an online newsletter. Her blog, *Seeking Green*, is part of the earth friendly food revolution.

Barbara Potter

Message from a Stranger

Searching through his tuxedo pockets, my husband glanced at me and said, "I can't find the parking ticket."

"Are you kidding me? That's all you had to be responsible for tonight," I said. "When you find it and our car is here, come inside and get me."

Stomping away on my high heels, I walked back inside, plopping into an overstuffed chair in front of a fireplace.

"I just want to go home," I mumbled to myself.

It had been a long evening. My week-long bout with the flu still hadn't finished its way through my body. I was tired and annoyed that I had to work Saturday night.

My friends think I have the best job. As a newspaper reporter I spend a lot of time at black-tie events interviewing celebrities as well as covering political issues and the news of the day. But this evening I did not want to get dressed up in my evening jacket, black dress pants and a too tight girdle. I wanted to be home sitting in my recliner wearing sweats, sipping tea and reading a book.

But here I was, waiting in the lobby of a five-star hotel having a pity-party. I couldn't seem to enjoy the beauty of the Pacific Ocean in the background or the 500 other people in evening attire. My ever-patient husband, Alan, had been listening to my complaints all evening while I worked the ballroom, getting quotes, and taking photographs for my newspaper story.

To add to my layer of impatience, we had been seated at a table with 10 other people where conversation wasn't possible during the four-course meal – next to us was a jumbo screen flashing a slide show and blasting music.

When the dinner and speeches were over, Alan and I quickly made our way to the entrance of the hotel, not bothering to stay to dance the night away.

While Alan figured out a way to get our mini-van without a ticket, I sat and waited. After a few minutes, a woman about my age, 60, walked by, turned and walked back.

"You look so lovely sitting there wearing that beautiful turquoise jacket," she said.

"Thank you," I said.

Hesitating for a second, she sat down in the other chair in front of the fireplace and started talking, her words spilling out, "I could have stayed home feeling sorry for myself, spending the evening crying, but I decided to be brave and come to this event by myself."

"Why? What do you mean?" I said.

"Six weeks ago my husband went out for his daily jog one morning, something he has done for years. He collapsed near our home and died; he was only 61 years old. I just can't believe it, and I miss him so much."

"Oh, I'm so sorry," I said as my eyes welled up.

"We had been married for 34 years and had the best marriage. We even worked together. We had such great plans for our retirement. I just can't believe he's gone. Are you married?"

"Yes, the same, 34 years."

Looking into my eyes, she said, "Love your husband with all your heart. Be good to him and treasure each moment with him. You never know when it will end."

In that instant, all my childish frustrations of the evening melted away.

Soon Alan walked up to me and said, "Your carriage awaits you, my dear."

When the three of us got to the entrance, I gave my new friend a hug. "Thank you so much for listening to me," she said. "You've helped me so much."

"Thank you for helping me," I said. I turned to Alan. "Sorry you had to wait."

"Oh, no problem," he said. "Actually it's kind of funny. The first car the valet brought me was a new car. Just think, we could have driven away in a new Mercedes."

As we pulled away from the hotel in our car, I looked at Alan and said, with tears spilling from my eyes, "I'm sorry I was so mean tonight. I love you."

BARBARA POTTER is an award-winning newspaper reporter, columnist, editor and a teacher of memoir writing. Author of *So She Says* and contributor to *Interstices, the Orange County Anthology*, she is currently editor of the *Laguna Woods Globe*, an *Orange County Register* community newspaper.

Everyone has talent. What is rare is the
courage to follow that talent to the dark
place where it leads.

— Erica Jong

NANCY RABBITT

All God's Creatures

I like to think that I have a "live and let live" attitude toward life in general and toward little lives too.

However, if you are a fly or a spider or a damselfly and I open the door for you and invite you outside, I shouldn't have to ask twice.

I have been known to capture small critters, especially spiders, in a jar and throw them outside. I'm always surprised they make a sound when they land. If I'm upstairs they are on their own cause I'm not doing the stairs for a spider and all the windows have screens.

I ought to mention here that the only thing I dislike more than uninvited guests is uninvited-guest poison spray. For pity's sake, we walk on that floor too!

Lately, we have had more flies than the Amityville house. Reason tells me that they are coming in through the sliders having hatched over at the horse stables. Clearly, they considered themselves too good to hang out for long there and looked for more refined accommodations. They seem to really enjoy the patio and the patio set with the umbrella covered table. It's like a little Meet-Up place for them.

You have a chance inviting one fly to leave but when they get that mob mentality it's a whole other story. So, I went to get some natural, doesn't-harm-children-or-pets flying insect spray. It does seem to help them fly and they may do a loop through the mist, which is quite impressive, but it's not the effect I hoped for. I have children, dogs, a parrot, a guinea pig and a husband to consider so I can't use anything stronger. *And* everyone complains about the spray's smell.

I just haven't figured out how to explain all this to human guests. I don't mean the children's behavior; I mean the bugs'. Sometimes – I have to admit – it's all out warfare and I want you to know that I do not send them on their heavenly journey without a little prayer or at least a "go see God."

There is a creek behind our house. We hear coyotes and see them too. We see rabbits, skunks, and raccoons. Recently, I asked a neighbor about the punishing tree trimming taking place next to her house and she told me that the raccoons were climbing the tree and scaring her children by staring at them through the windows on the roof. That's a twist on children peering out.

Every summer there is a portion of the creek area that gets mowed when the grass turns brown. This is a signal for the mice to pack their little bags and head north. If they can make it alive across the street, and they all seem to, they must see a little sign on my back fence that says "kind woman leaves water and dog food free for the taking." They really like Kirkland's lamb and rice.

These mice are not like any others I have ever seen. They have Dumbo ears set low on their heads. Are they mutants? I don't know. It does raise the question of the well water quality in my mind.

Their presence in the house was the last straw. I went down to Denault's Hardware and bought the strongest rodent killing poison cakes I could find. I placed them in strategic locations around the kitchen including in the cabinet under the sink. I forgot my daughter thought it was clever to teach our dogs to open doors. One day I came home to find a gnawed poison cake on the stairs.

My husband had passed by it earlier and "wondered" what it was. He has his own philosophy about don't ask, don't tell. Don't ask if this wool sweater can go in the washer. Don't tell that I used your best bath towel to clean up a grape juice spill. Don't mention that our son fell off his bike, chipped a tooth, and now has a severe headache. He thinks this philosophy will keep him from getting yelled at but he is sooooo wrong.

Did I say that I have three small dogs – any one of which could be the rat-poison-chewing, cupboard-door-opening culprit? I called the vet and he told me to bring them down right away. I stuffed them all into a small dog crate – you can do that with Chihuahuas – and I took them down. I apologized to them for what was about to happen. Two of them were innocent, I was sure. My dogs were fine. The vet was happy to tell me that he thought he got everything up from their stomachs even carrots. They do like raw carrots. It was only $150 for that information.

I did not relent in my waged war on Rodentville. I just made sure that the poison biscuits were well out of reach of my pets. The mice obliged me by eating the stuff and not chewing through the dishwasher water line like they did once before prompting a service call expense and leaking under the sink. In the all out battle they have gotten their licks in too. My husband was then able to bring his <u>one</u> unsprung mousetrap down from the attic.

Writing about this has raised my ire. This is my house, dammit. They can all go find their own places to live. I just wish they weren't so darn cute. Then I could live without guilt for the (sometimes) unavoidable chemical warfare.

The insects are not cute but still they are all God's creatures so they will get at least one invitation to leave with the door held open before they are dearly departed. For that I am sorry, but they can't cross my path and live here for long. I do hope my now adult age children take note.

NANCY RABBITT, MFA, a watercolorist, "sometime" poet and writer, teacher, prior business owner, EFT energy healer/trainer and empath, is part of the *Writer's Circle* in San Juan Capistrano. http://nancyrabbitt@blogspot.com

Something of vengeance I had tasted for the first time; as aromatic wine it seemed, on swallowing, warm and racy: its after-flavor, metallic and corroding, gave me a sensation as if I had been poisoned.

— Charlotte Bronte

Breaking Apart

She froze, fork poised inches from her salad. The conversation had started out like any other. But then he said, "Sara, I…" and then paused, his eyes full, and he got her undivided attention. A fleeting, yet absurd, thought surfaced: *why did he choose the corner cafe for such a momentous occasion?*

She was dead wrong about the "momentous occasion." Once he said there was "someone else," the rest of his words fell flat, stale clichés like "you deserve better" and "I'm not ready." She was acutely aware of her pulse throbbing behind an eyeball. The periphery of her vision blurred as she watched his hand slide her condo key instead of an engagement ring across the table. She automatically whispered thank you. He told her he'd stopped by that morning after she had already gone to work to get his "stuff." She nodded, but she was conscious only of that pulse in her right eye. Was it speeding up?

Later, as they left half eaten lunches – she in stunned silence, he in relief and perhaps shame – the café owner gave them a small wave and smile, as always, and everything seemed so normal. A part of her looked on, a curious and impartial observer, but a persistent refrain surfaced somewhere in her mind whispering…*this will be the last time.*

That evening, the phone rang and she held her breath as she answered. When a telemarketer stumbled over the pronunciation of her name, she surprised herself by saying *fuck you* as she slammed down the receiver. Her meanness made her gasp, and that's when the sobbing started. After a few minutes, she listened to herself and she sounded like a walrus barking; it was awful and embarrassing. Even so, she almost giggled since she felt so outside herself. Her first thought was to call and tell him. He would think it funny too, *he would have thought*, she corrected herself.

At work the next day, she made several mistakes and then corrected them without telling anyone. She walked into her desk three times, badly bruising her thigh, spilled coffee on a file and bumped her head on the shelves near the printer. It was a solid smack that brought tears to her eyes. One of the clerks looked up, but Sara just half-smiled as the knot formed on her skull. By evening, along with the bruised thigh and lump on her head, her chest felt as if she had swallowed a rock.

Friday night loomed long and empty. When she opened the hall closet to hang her coat, she caught sight of his jogging shoes carelessly intertwined with her own. Without thinking, she grabbed the shoes, hurried to her car, and drove toward his apartment.

Leaving the shoes on the doorstep was too sad; knocking on the door, saying she was passing by – too desperate. She should have contemplated calling first or maybe sending email or a text to set up a time to deliver the shoes, a time when he was sure to be home. It all seemed too complicated.

Heart racing as she slowly approached his street, she imagined him opening the door and falling into her arms. He would confess the break-up had been a huge mistake. They'd go out for Friday night crepes and things would be as before.

Lights from his kitchen windows illuminated the chrome on his motorcycle out front. Wildly optimistic when she found a parking space, she moved quickly, willing herself not to over-think everything the way he claimed. It was a cool night, but she felt feverish as she got out of the car.

Shoes in hand, she froze as she heard voices and recognized his soft, lilting laugh. There he was in the shadows, walking with his arm around a girl to a double-parked Volkswagen. The couple got in and the girl drove, her blonde hair catching the moonlight. Mute, Sara could not move as she cradled his shoes in her arms.

He had passed by so closely that she could smell the memory of his leather jacket in the night air, but he hadn't even noticed her. She had been invisible.

She leaned against his motorcycle, clutching the shoes. *Breathe*. Putting one hand to her chest as if to stop a bleeding wound, she touched the motorcycle's smooth chrome with the other. She had felt so free when she rode behind him.

Reaching for her keys in her pocket, hands trembling, she opened the small

Swiss Army knife on her key ring – a gift from him, in case of an "emergency." Crouching, she jabbed the sharp blade into the rear tire as hard as she could. Once the incision was made, her vision sharpened, her hearing became alert to every sound, and she was fully aware, alive. Adrenaline pumping, she wrenched the knife out of the tire and heard the satisfying hiss of deflation.

Clutching the shoes, she ran back to her car. Ravenous when she got home, she made pasta with garlic bread and poured herself a large glass of cabernet. Her heightened taste buds made every bite exquisite.

Days passed and there was no angry phone call about the punctured tire. She began to walk around with her right hand lightly pressed against her sternum as if holding her heart in place. A co-worker offered a Tums. The jogging shoes remained on the floor of her car.

Another weekend came and went. Three weeks after he had slid the key across the table, she came home to find a note on her door. She felt a flutter in her chest when she saw his familiar writing. "Stopped by for my shoes. Call me. R"

Over her second glass of wine, she picked up the phone, but hung up. Staring at the note, she waited, but the relaxation she expected from the wine didn't come. Instead, she felt lean, angry and brittle, like a twig ready to snap.

In the small backyard, she mourned the unfinished patio. The rustic red bricks they had carefully selected from Home Depot still waited to be artfully placed for the planter. They'd talked of a small wedding on the deck in late summer.

She set her wine glass down, snatched a couple of bricks from the pile, returned to the house for her keys, and hurried out to her car. The sun had set and the moon had yet to rise.

Once on his street, she noticed his motorcycle gone and his kitchen windows dark. She parked in an illegal spot while she shoved a brick into each of his expensive jogging shoes. She tied the laces into neat bows and sat with the weight of the shoes balanced on her lap.

How easy it was to imagine the window glass shattering, breaking apart with a shocking crash, the shoes lying on the floor on the other side, clearly identifying her as the vandal. Briefly, she considered writing a note, something vulgar or cruel, or maybe she should just write: *It's me!*

Carrying the shoes up the path, she checked the air for the scent of his leather jacket. There was nothing but jasmine. She hadn't even noticed the change of seasons, how the nights had become heavy and warm.

She placed the shoes neatly side by side on the doorstep, breathed deeply of the jasmine, and turned around to walk back to her car. In her head she heard the echo of her own thoughts – *this will be the last time*.

———◆———

TRACY KNOX is a lawyer living in San Francisco. She enjoys writing short fiction and has never committed any acts of vandalism. Another story by this author appears in the Encore section.

Nostalgic Journey

It was that small square step stool the sleeping car attendant placed on the concrete platform below the open door of the Santa Fe Chief, which took me back many years to rolling trips in Pullman cars with my mother and younger brother. From Olympia, Washington, to Akron, Ohio, the trip was three days and three nights and we braved it every summer to stay with Mother's father and sister.

Or, perhaps I should say, our mother braved it. Jerry and I loved all of it: the making up of the berths, the curtains which enclosed them, the dining car with fingerbowls and doilies under the china place settings, the swinging vestibules between cars, the smoky observations car, and the friendly Pullman porters.

Here I was again, after more than sixty years, ready to step onto a passenger train and embark on an adventure. It was a steamy July afternoon in Galesburg, Illinois, a small edge-of-the-prairie town southeast of Davenport, Iowa. My husband and I had driven along I-74 for eight hours from our home in western Ohio and parked our minivan in the Amtrak station lot, arriving two hours early just in case. The woman stationmaster issued us paper tickets, purchased on the Internet weeks before, and assured us that parking was free for the duration of our journey. At least five major freight trains passed the Galesburg Station while we sat outside in the shade.

As we waited, twenty senior Boy Scouts arrived, clad in their short sleeve, badge-encrusted uniform shirts which topped an amazing variety of non-regulation shorts. Parents took many group photos until a voice on the public address system announced that the Chief would soon be coming down the track from Chicago, which caused all of us to gather our luggage and move along to the boarding area. Excitement was in the air as we continued to wait another ten minutes for the sound of the train whistle.

The Scouts climbed aboard the lounge car near the front of the train. Several hours later we learned that they were joining 150 other senior Scouts headed for northern New Mexico, some to get off at the high Raton Pass and set out on a backpacking expedition, some for an encampment.

Handing my suitcase to the car attendant and hoisting my small carry-on over my shoulder, I put one foot on the step stool and accepted the challenge of climbing the high step into the last car. I wondered briefly if I had been lifted into the train by one of the Pullman porters during my early journeys. But a steep, winding staircase leading to the upper floor required all my attention this time, and I was soon standing next to our pint-size roomette. Two lounge chairs faced each other over a small table with a large window beyond gracing the entire outer wall.

We would later discover that the lounge chairs became a cozy two-by-six-foot lower bunk while the pull-down upper one was slightly smaller. There was room to hang several pieces of clothing and stow two overnight kits. A sliding door, heavy curtains, or both provided privacy from the narrow aisle and the roomette across from ours. The half bath was four roomettes away.

As the Chief's whistle sounded departure and we moved out of Galesburg to begin our 23-hour journey to Albuquerque, the car attendant took down our desired time for supper in the dining car and noted the coffee and juice always available in our sleeper car.

Soon I was relearning the art of balancing on a moving train as we made our way through the other sleeper cars and several swinging vestibules to share a dining table with two interesting people. And for the rest of the trip I moved a number of times between our roomette, the dining car, and the observation car enjoying meeting a number of fellow passengers, including a lone senior Scout who had been on trains two days coming from New England, a mother and junior high boy traveling to a family reunion out west because the boy's ear problems prevented him from flying, and dinner companions who had boarded in Kansas City, Missouri, and who knew, in that city, the daughter of our former Cincinnati neighbors.

I took a book to read in the observation car, but I hardly made it through ten pages the whole trip because of the magnificent scenery and people who wanted to talk.

I didn't sleep much that first night, traveling south. Even the lulling rhythm of the train couldn't overcome my interest in watching the activity at each stop as passengers stepped on and off aided by other step stools and train attendants. I was glad to be on the side where I could see them and also follow the course of the moon, nearly full on the distant horizon.

After ten days in New Mexico, as I stepped down onto a small square step stool back in Galesburg, I reflected what a community a train trip becomes, in vivid contrast to today's air travel.

JOYCE VAN BUSKIRK CAUFFIELD has written non-technical articles for a San Francisco trade journal publishing company, edited a variety of newsletters, coached elementary students doing creative writing and articles for school newspapers, and created, with historian Carolyn Banfield, *The River Book: Cincinnati and the Ohio* containing articles by a variety of Ohio River experts and enthusiasts as well as a profusion of photographs.

*Art is a shutting in in order to shut out. Art is a
ritualistic binding of the perpetual motion machine that
is nature... Art is spellbinding. Art fixes the audience
in its seat, stops the feet before a painting, fixes a book
in the hand. Contemplation is a magic act.*

— Camille Paglia

LAURIE RICHARDS

Last and Perfect

Before the firmament, before the cosmos, before all time and sound began, the Almighty existed, ageless and omnificent.

And bored.

He slumbered.

When he woke, his yawn – a blasting breath – created the winds. With another yawn, he expelled the universe in a burst of light. He sneezed, stared at a round splotch he had set into the cosmos and shrugged.

I'll call that Earth, he thought, and he walked as a zephyr upon Earth, not quite so bored. For a billion years.

Then he dreamed of heat and sparked his dream into a living flame that swayed before him in worship.

I shall create sound and name this being, he thought. He breathed one word to the flame. "George," he said, and his voice poured over Earth and suffocated the flame. The Almighty left its ashes in the dust.

He rested again for a billion years and let the water of life ooze around him. He gathered it, shaped it, willed it into a living form that spread before him. *I shall name it*, he thought. *It is my right*.

"George," he said, and the living water sizzled at the sound, sizzled, boiled and evaporated, its remains a dried blotch in the dust. The Almighty looked at the blotch and shrugged.

He took a break.

After another billion years, he decided to try air. He blew winds into a living whirl that spun and bowed before him.

"George?" he said, and the twirling wind collapsed.

Another billion years passed.

I have it, the Almighty thought. He gathered dust from the suffocated flame, from the collapsed whirlwind, from the dried ooze, and he shaped it all, gave it a cochlea and a larynx and lots of bones. So that it could hear and speak and stand before him.

I shall name it for the adamah, the dust from which it came, he thought and whispered to the shape, "Adam?"

Adam smiled.

That worked well, thought the Almighty. And he set to making other things. Things that crawled and flew and climbed and swam and slithered. Things that grew from roots, great blooming things that fruited.

Adam watched and smiled.

But the Almighty didn't name his new creations. *It would be too boring, and I'm due for a nap.* He whispered low to Adam, "Thou art unique in all the cosmos, my Adam."

Adam smiled, and the Almighty willed Adam's gaze to fall upon all the living things created. "Name them," he said. "I give to thee my gift of the Word." And, content with the delegation, the Almighty fell into slumber.

A billion years passed. When the Almighty awoke, he called to Adam in his soft voice. "Hast thou finished the task I set you?"

Adam nodded, smiling.

"Good," said the Almighty. "Parade them before me and, when they pass, speak the name of each."

The living things gathered, and as they marched, Adam pointed at them, one by one and spoke.

"Word," Adam said as a great beast lumbered past. "Word," he said again, but pointed to tiny furred creatures.

"Word . . .word," he said as things on twos and fours scurried before them.

The Almighty stared at Adam, not watching the things on sixes and eights and hundreds passing by.

"Word," said Adam over and over. Crawling things came into view, and Adam spoke again. "Word –"

"For God's sake, stop." The Almighty forgot to whisper, and Adam fell to the ground and cowered before his creator.

The Almighty reached out and patted Adam's head. "It is not thy fault, but mine. Thou hast spent too much time alone. I shall sleep on it," he said, and he slumbered.

For a few minutes.

I need a checklist more than a nap, he decided.

"Word?" said Adam.

One. Needs to be more creative, the Almighty thought.

He watched Adam, who watched the words – especially when they joined their bodies to make new words. Adam stared and did nothing else.

Two. Needs to think a little less about joining bodies.

He commanded Adam, "Go into the west away from the words and sleep while I ponder."

Adam headed east.

Three. Needs to ask for directions.

When Adam awoke and returned, the Almighty watched him stare again at the joined words, and Adam walked as he stared and touched himself as he walked. And then he tripped.

Needs to multi-task, thought the Almighty. *That's four.*

"Stupid words," Adam said, wiping red ooze from his knee.

Needs compassion. Five.

Adam watched the joining words again and touched himself until he shuddered, then slept.

The Almighty regarded the sleeping Adam. *Needs more energy after whatever was going on there.* He stroked his beard, and an idea filled him.

From the dark the Almighty formed the purple hues of evening, and, under cover of the night, he took a rib from Adam who snored and sniffled in his sleep. "Word," Adam called out from his slumber.

Seven. Needs more brain.

The Almighty sighed with exhaustion. He reviewed his checklist, and, waving Adam's rib through the purple hues he had formed, he created another being and looked upon the supple form before him.

"I shall name you for the evening from whence you came."

"Lovely," she said.

The Almighty nodded, and a breeze arose and blew softly through her hair. He pointed to the things on fours and sixes and eights and bellies and so on. "Name them," he said.

She smiled. "No problem." She stretched out her hand to the things passing before her. "Jaguar, flamingo, tarantula. . ."

This may be my last creation, thought the Almighty.

"One favor," he said to her, and his Eve from soft and purple hues paused. The

Almighty glanced toward Adam on the ground, dreaming his dreams.

"I know," she said. "Let him think it was all his idea."

"Perfect," said the Almighty.

And then he slumbered.

LAURIE RICHARDS is an attorney who would rather be writing. She's a writing instructor for the Extended Learning Institute, California State University San Marcos, and she lectures on writing tips for the Pasadena Library System. She authors articles on "Revision Tips" for the San Diego Writers and Editors Guild. Laurie is the Judging Chair of the Short Story Category for the San Diego Book Awards. She's published short stories and garnered several awards for her fiction. She's working on novels that take place in 1930s Kansas and present-day Georgia.

People have talents that are different. Where does the creative flow come from – inside us, or from a higher power! I don't ask any questions. I just write it down.

— Phyllis Whitney

KATHLEEN D. SIMPSON

Thirteen Weeks

There you are,
afloat
in an amniotic sea
smaller than
a butterfly fish
spine – a coral branch,
heart pulsing,
shining through
murky water
like bioluminescence
in spring.

I watch
you pivot onto your back
and see your face,
profile chiseled
with your mother's nose,
father's brow
ascending as familiar
as Polaris.

Some say
once
we were all fish
and that is why
you swim awhile
inside your mother's womb,
frolic among her tides,
awaken to the rhythms
of her heart
while you decide
to be or not to be.

I say
someone
dreamed you
from dust of countless stars.
You may be dreaming now
of voyages
beneath constellations
above rivers bright
with moonlight.

❖

Invisibility

We had been friends for thirty years and so her comment didn't offend me. Waiting for our husbands to retrieve the car after dinner at an upscale restaurant, we caught ourselves looking down at our clearly downscale shoes. The toe of hers was unfashionably square, the heel short and clunky. I was wearing a black lace up sport shoe, the only style that would accommodate the orthotics recently prescribed for my tendonitis.

"Oh well," she said, "it's not like anyone's looking at us."

Although her comment brought on a protracted case of the giggles, there was something about it that pierced through the humor, a quick insect sting, a bug bite. I began to feel an old irritation, a bump of annoyance wanting to be scratched. Looking around the room I noticed that yes, indeed, we were the oldest women there by at least two decades. We were not wearing skirts that ended at the thigh. We didn't own boots that climbed above the knee. What cleavage we had was last seen in public during the first term of the Reagan administration. I had thought of myself as entirely comfortable in my sagging skin. So why would my friend's comment prickle?

A decade or so ago, I began to notice a gravitational shift in the sphere of my everyday wanderings. It was subtle at first, fleeting. I would be browsing through clothes in a store, glad at first to be left alone, when an obviously younger, more stylish woman would enter and immediately be approached by the salesperson with an offer to assist. Or I would be out with my daughters, then in college, in a coffee shop, a theater, or sporting event. Common courtesies such as doors held open, seating offered, a parcel carried, would be extended readily to them, always by males, and I would be not so much disregarded, as in rudely treated, but simply unseen, as in disembodied. I began to notice that at cocktail parties the small talk was becoming so small that I considered slipping a book into my purse (these were the days before e-books) and sneaking off to the powder room.

When I was a teenager, back in the early days of rock n' roll, the Cold War, and drive-in movies, modesty for girls was considered a virtue. Conceit, according to the nuns who were my teachers, was considered a sin. At the very least, calling undue attention to oneself in public was considered very bad manners. Still I learned, along with my girlfriends, that we were, in fact, in possession of a power, a force field, an almost magical, nearly mystical energy particular to our gender.

From puberty on, we learned how to manipulate this power, to become comfortable with it, to use it not only to attract, but just as easily to repel. We could, at will, repel any boy we didn't want pursuing us as easily as we could attract some of the boys whose attention we desired. This skill set worked just as well with girls as we constructed the social hierarchies of adolescence. For all of our allegiance during our college years to the feminist tenet of being valued for our brains, we readily engaged with our female sexual power in all of its liberated intensity. We befriended it. We wore it as we pleased, sometimes flamboyantly, other times demurely, always with a sense of individuality. Marriage and motherhood only increased our confidence, defining our visibility in the larger world as symbols of fertility and commerce.

And so it was shocking to wake up one day and find that something had been altered in the world. That reliable female magnetism, source of so much joy, so much pain, had alchemically changed and drifted out of the atmosphere like volcanic ash. And in its place emerged a fully formed, flush faced, newly incarnated Crone. Some women I know found themselves depressed in this new reality, others found that they were angry. There was talk of surgical procedures. There were divorces. For many of us, the rooms of our homes had grown silent, the children we had devoted so many years of our lives to vanished, away to school or beginning career paths. And in the workplace, younger men and women fresh from those schools arrived with new knowledge, new skills, and a future.

Much has been written about the change of life and about the medical and emotional issues associated with it. But I don't recall, in all of Crone Wisdom and Lore, any practical solutions, any consoling songs, to guide the once confident woman of presence through the mists of disconnection, of invisibility. There aren't even shoes fit to wear for this journey. Perhaps the reason is that this is a temporary state, a necessary state. Day by day, week by week, following the initial trauma, the body and mind once again become allies; the wraithlike energy begins to coalesce. And if "no one is looking at us" as my friend has reminded me, it is because so many people are now "looking to us."

I remember so well, back when my children were in elementary school, thinking ahead into the distant future of a day in my life with no swim meets, no dance classes, no PTA, carpools or schedules. Later I looked forward to nights without watching the clock, pacing the floor, worrying about teenage drivers and unchaperoned parties. Those years came and went so quickly. And despite the fact that for many years my children wished that I were invisible, my visibility was high and capricious. As it is again now that those children have given birth to my four grandchildren. To my great delight, since my elevation to the status of progenitor and foremother, I am often sought for my expertise in sustaining these highly intelligent, beautifully behaved, organically fed and gifted offspring. At the same time, my spouse of forty years has discovered that I have become so in tune with his wishes and needs as to be telepathic. I am blessed with a living parent, and as the oldest daughter I attend to her often, even though she resides in a different state. And there are friends, dear friends, a circle of women supporting each other in our efforts to remain healthy, vibrant, and relevant to the world. We are at each other's sides when our best efforts fail us, when we or our families endure illness or loss.

There is a time that I remember, shortly after my daughters' college graduations, of balance, equilibrium, and a sense of being settled in my life, of having completed a phase of large and important responsibility. I don't recall being particularly visible in the world during that time, but neither do I remember being invisible. Some psychologists and self-help authors have referred to this interlude as a time of "post-menopausal zest." But I don't remember being zesty. I don't know what I did with those years, in a focused way. Yes, I traveled, read books, took some classes. But I wish that I had lived those years with the same sense of urgency that I feel today, with the same passion for the people who comprise my life, for the causes and beliefs that give it meaning.

"Oh well," my friend said, "it's not like anyone is looking at us."

Would I ever have believed, back in my twenties, thirties, forties, that this truth, in reflection, would be a reason for gratitude, a cause for celebration? The years of visibility come with a price. They never go on sale. I have learned that to be visible within the cultural feminine stereotype of modern America is to be coerced into a state of self-centeredness as opposed to a condition of self-consciousness. Invisible, I no longer feel compelled to waste time in the pursuit of someone else's unattainable goals. No longer do I engage in the self centered, chaotic activities that serving these goals entails. Over the years my female friends and I have learned together that nurturing the self, rather than indulging the ego, means being embraced by women and men who honor our talents, our spirit, our love.

Every woman I know embodies this nurturing so effortlessly in their relationships with their grandchildren. Maybe the reason that our grandchildren, especially the small ones, express such joy in us and request so often to be in our company is because we are among the first people to open our arms to them, to carry them atop our shoulders where their view of the world is enlarged. We honor them in rhyme and song, we allow them to hide from us, we allow them to be found. We tell them stories about the people who came before them. We celebrate them and their place in our families while they are still largely invisible in the world.

My granddaughter has just turned six years old. There is only one style of shoe that she is willing to wear to school, a white leather tennis shoe with Velcro fasteners instead of laces. She wants to wear these shoes because this is the style that most of her female classmates have chosen. How can I convince her that the only shoes worth wearing are the shoes that will support her own growing feet? She already knows that everyone is looking at her.

———————◆——————

KATHLEEN SIMPSON has been published in *Good Housekeeping*, *Los Angeles Times*, *The Houston Chronicle*, and other national and regional publications. A member of *The Writing Well*, she was recently selected to attend the Napa Valley Writers' Conference poetry workshop.

APRIL HAMATAKE

The Red Kimono

In this dream, this mirror
you wear a red kimono
your hair black like the rain
at night in Kalihi Valley.

Dusty perfume bottles exhale
memories of ylang ylang blossoms,
Shalimar, Bal a Versailles,
the red kimono
its black and white yinyang swirls,
loosely draped over
your still moist breasts
your belly, stretchmarked with tallies
of your babies,

My five-year-old eyes
memorizing you, imagining
eyebrows I would draw,
lips I would pucker
rouge I would streak across moist cheeks
a daughter who would sit at my knee,
handmirror held to her ear
the echo of herself
bouncing back and forth
between the large mirror,
the small mirror,
down the long hall of faces,
me looking at you,
your face, my face,

your child, my child
one long chain of eyes.

Ten years later I took
the red kimono, limp
from your bed,
so red it made my eyes burn
I buried it in a banker's box
in my closet through years
of black ice and bluebirds,

I stand in your red kimono
my black hair drizzling,
down my back.

———◆—

APRIL HAMATAKE, a resident of Chapel Hill, NC, is a licensed body-worker who enjoys lomi lomi, artmaking, and painting. Originally from Hawaii, she has written through several states and back again. She is one of the original members of the *Writing Well* based in Corona del Mar.

SHERRILL ERICKSON

Her Address to the Ladies, correction: Women's Bar Association
By Mrs. Hapenny Thud

Today she will give a speech at the Women's Bar Association luncheon. Speech is not the right word. Speech connotes podium. Connotes church pulpit. Connotes Gettysburg address.

She will give a talk. She will not "give" anything in fact. She will lead a discussion. A discussion about Women's *Issues*. The female attorneys at law issues. Issues connotes – tissues. Toilet tissue. Tissues connotes – crying or wiping, or amorphous internal slime. Connotes "therapy". Issues is not right. Issues connotes – the menstrual cycle.

She will not lead a discussion. She will not lead anything. Lead connotes leash. Connotes dog. Connotes man. Connotes lifting a leg.

She in fact will *share* some of her thoughts. Share some of her experiences. Some of her perceptions. Sharing connotes caring. Caring connotes nurturing. Nurturing connotes motherhood. Motherhood connotes woman. Connotes clinging, sobbing, bleeding menstrual effluent.

She will *explore*. No, she will explain. Elucidate. Illuminate. No, illuminate connotes mysticism. Connotes religion. Connotes self-help guru. Connotes therapy. Connotes woman. And issues tissues etcetera.

This is it. She will list. That is all. She will list and point. Point out tactics. Tactical maneuvers. Very good. Connotes war. Connotes man. Connotes stealth. Connotes hunting. Connotes killing. Connotes victory. A legal victory. A battle won. Tactics of the game of winning. Winning at law. Winning cases. Beating the opponent. Hating and beating the opponent. For the spoils. For the material goods. The king of the hill. The survivor. The victor and the vanquished. Tactics to become the victor. Clever catalogues of rules, and how to manipulate the rules to one's advantage. *One's decided advantage*. That is what the brain is for, isn't it? That is what evolution is all about. To get the advantage. Any. Way. You. Can.

The problem is that she, in a moment of hormonally induced ovulatory confidence, actually called the Women's Bar Association President and chatted her up casually and thereafter confidently agreed to *lead* a discussion about an *issue* unique to female lawyers. This is what her attempts at networking resulted in. Her doing some chore for someone. Some chore that seems as light as a feather when agreed to, but ultimately becomes heavy as a dragging lead cannon ball. Like the heavy aching menstruation that she feels is imminent, now, immediately prior to her luncheon address.

She wants to lie down and be quiet. Lie down in a dark cave with no sound but a cricket. A single cricket. But instead she will be tossed in the boiling insect chatter of attorneys. Attorneys who are decidedly female and aggressive talkers and discerners and game players. Only that kind. The quiet studious attorneys will not come to some barbarous luncheon of women trying to be men. Who even uses the word luncheon anymore? That ought to be a red flag right there. And now with a few more gadgets like cell phones and palm things about them to gabble and gobble incessantly with . . .

With their powers of detection. Yea, with the hairs in their quivering nostrils they will detect, will they not, the chemical reality of her state. The diminution of pheromones associated with the change in estrogen, yea she will not be quick with a come back. Her sparkle will be fraudulent, concealing dullness, an ache, and a flow of blood, softness, a wound, and a weakness. A girlness. A terrible guilt weighing her down to the bottom of the sea.

Oh, don't kid yourself that only females will attend. Far from it. The usual fags will be there. A certain G in his immaculate little get-up. Fresh from his stylist. His head will be shaved perfectly. Such perfect short hair. And that very fine ring of hair around his mouth. A work of art. Totally symmetrical. A miracle really. He is one of those virtuosi of the fastidious toilette. A clever and deceptively urbane and witty talker. A favorite at these kinds of functions. But a gossip. Spreading the kind of gossip that seeps in

154

masquerading as caring and sharing. He will love to *share* his *concern* about someone else's problem, about her obvious problem, will he not?

Then there will be the momma's boy tagalongs. Inevitably dumpy and dull, nodding their heads, shoveling in food. Food from mother. Sex is out. But food is fine. The breast. The blessed silence of the breast. Any breast. Gargantuan or plastic. Flat or fuliginous. Pert or drooping. Warm food in mouth equals boobs.

Now for the *issue*, the topic of the day. It must be the discussion of a new or amended statute, ordinance, or rule. Perhaps some federal mandate flowing in vast waves of paper to every outpost of civilization. And in dry precision she will read the inevitably long and piteously dull statute, boring even herself into a stupor. Scratching herself like a gauche simian. Read it and then announce that it was amended effective on such and such date and that it will not be retroactive. Then she will ask for comments. And the little swarm will buzz this way and that way and then it will be over. She will be so dull and predictable, she will not even be gossiped about. Just digested and forgotten. Cut to: beatific Buddha smile or proboscis of tapir rummaging, snuffing in mud under logs for termites.

She need not be gay and beautiful. She need not be charming. She need not have dazzling lips, shining eyes. She need only read the rule. Better if she puts on spectacles. Not merely glasses. Not "cool" shades. Something heavy with a chain on it. Or a *pince nez*. No. Something she can fumble for, be helpless without. And then she should clear her throat and simply laboriously read the language of the statute verbatim. That is all.

A joke would be okay. A natural sounding joke. A joke about herself would be excellent. But a joke is a matter of careful timing, a matter of genuine lightheartedness. A joke can fall flat. She has seen it happen. In fact, it has happened to her more than once. So forget the joke.

Now it would be nice to glimmer with mischief and produce a joke, i.e., *crack* a joke. As easy and natural as cracking a . . . never mind.

But again it is a matter of timing and elocution. One cannot tell even the best joke with a melancholy demeanor. A sad sack can tell a joke about being sad, but only if she is not truly sad. If she is truly sad, her sadness will drown the joke. She will be a "wet blanket" so to speak.

If she prepared a joke and practiced and practiced, she might be able to deliver it properly and achieve the desired effect, i.e., laughter. But a joke must flow from the circumstances one finds oneself in. She is not after all a stand-up comedienne. Well, she could be, at least enough to deliver a single solitary two-second joke, and excuses are unacceptable. For this is a game; it must be won. Victor and vanquished. And she must play the game, calculate, and play aggressively, and try to win. Is she an attorney at law, or merely bleeding and wanting to lie down, to nestle, to nest with tissues, issues etc.

Now if she were ovulating, instead of menstruating, and if she were – say – in a strip club. Say she was a topless dancer in a thong, say in Thailand, and if she were seventeen, instead of forty-seven, she would not be clearing her throat, fumbling for spectacles, and reading the amended Rule 54(b) of Civil Procedure, with no nod and wink, no joke, no tiny snicker like air released, gas released, pressure released, from an over-inflated tire.

Hypothetically speaking, of course, she would in that instance, the instance of being a Bangkok dancer at seventeen, be wrapping paper money around her middle F-you finger. She wouldn't look at the crowd when it was her turn to climb the stairs, to get in the lit cage, to show what she was. And she would be what she was, Rule 54 notwithstanding.

Her dancing would be far superior to the others and she would know that. Because hers would be body and soul. Not devised to manipulate, to be a commercial exchange. What she wanted them to witness was something. What they saw was something else. So she would shove them over and dump them over and kick them over and throw them out of there. Out of the inner sacred place, the penetrailia. The pure place. Of feeling. Of being alive in your own skin.

In the gardenia breath evening, ice cream cone fallen melting on the still warm sunset gumshoe sidewalk, beach scented ocean molecules, leaning against the doorway, her tray in hand, lithe hip cocked. Last ray of the sun, orange in her eye. She was a girl. You could see her ribcage. She hadn't even started menstruating.

SHERRILL ERICKSON is an attorney and a real estate broker living on the Big Island of Hawaii. She enjoys riding and jumping her horses as well as creative pursuits, such as music, art, and writing. Another story by this author appears in the Encore section.

Writing, which is my form of celebration
and prayer, is also my form of inquiry.

— Diane Ackerman

LORAINE FERRARA

Roadie

She was the one who swaddled the cymbals in lambs wool,
packed the guitars away in velvet cases
loosened drumheads to rest.

Had a whole system to classify the cords and cables
speakers, mikes, amplifiers
"Where's the –"
She already knew.

After the show, when the boys
took comfort in strange beds or
sweet smoke
She stayed on, heard chairs clapping
ate cold popcorn, dished with
the lighting techs.

Then loading the truck just so,
She'd spread out the sleeping bag,
lock the doors and sleep
among these her lovers, her children.

At fifteen with hips as straight as a cracker-box
her chest a flapper's dream
the old women clucked
"Best put her in secretarial classes,
at least that way –

❖

Agawam River

Walking there, down past the Agawam River to the place where it meets the Connecticut; was that River Road? I don't remember ever actually touching that shore, but I do remember the bridge that went over past Dunkin' Donuts where Mr. Macy worked, a small rectangular hat on his head, his lean body turned towards the grease, his face turned away, smiling eyes, a kindness towards us children, that's what I remember.

Over the bridge to West Springfield where the apartment was, the apartment where my parents had lived; I think it was called The West Springfield Gardens but I don't remember it – my father would say, *of course you remember living there, when we had the old Buick and I would say, Dad, I was 18 months old –*

Across the street the Eastern States Exposition, each State with its own building – Maple syrup in the Vermont building, Massachusetts with the cranberry bouncing machine, Maine with lobsters probably, by the time I got to Rhode Island I was bored and wanted to get cotton candy, go on rides, see the cows nuzzling each other in the warm barns rich with dust and fur and milk and feed.

It lit up at night, and the lights would reflect all around, I thought it was the best thing, fall and New England and the maples screaming their colors, and soon it would be my mother's birthday which meant cake from the Venetian Bakery, and then ten days later my birthday which meant another cake from the Venetian bakery – an almost continuous cake supply for *days.*

Then Columbus day, which I didn't know was politically incorrect then, it was a day off from school with parades and pastrami sandwiches, and Columbus was Italian so of course I was proud.

Then came Halloween, with my red gypsy costume, then the first frost, and Pilgrims and all colors of corn and woven stalks and pumpkin everything before Thanksgiving and the first snow. Macy's Thanksgiving Day parade, even in black and white I was mesmerized, then the snow would start in earnest, driving me to the basement to make Christmas wreaths of macaroni or turkey feathers.

The river would freeze, the cutters would come through to break up the ice. By Christmas, the river and everything around it was silent and white.

❖

ROY G BIV

A simple way to remember the colors of the color wheel is by using the mnemonic ROY G BIV, with R standing for red, O for orange and so forth. – Glynnis Beckwith, in How to Understand Color

I don't remember where we got the paint. Left over from someone's project someplace. But Deb took ROY and I took BIV and Justin refused to limit himself.

We spread the newspapers around the old Coke machine, sanded it down a bit, and Deb went to work on the south side – the sunny side, painting Kokopelli in every shade and hue of ROY and accenting him with Saguaro cactus, which in Arkansas is an exotic plant. Here and there, she'd add a woman collecting plants in the desert, or children playing, but mostly it was Kokopelli playing his flute, over and over.

On the north side, I created the midnight sky – Aurora Borealis, shooting stars, with Venus and Mars conjunct and Jupiter trining. Using the faded red and white ribbon logo on the bottom of the machine, I worked it into dusk, then progressed until the top of the machine was blue-black.

Justin went post-modern, painting the squares behind the drink choices in primary colors, then did a geometric around the coin slot and the enclosure where the cans came out. It was perfect. Move over, Kandinsky.

It was just something to do, to brighten the place up. But word got out about the "crazy Coke machine" and it became a destination. There's not much to do in Fayetteville after school lets out and besides, we were just a few blocks away from George's Majestic Lounge, with its ongoing supply of musicians, dancers, and slightly drunk people. It was nothing for me to awaken at three AM with a gaggle of artists dropping quarters both in the machine and on the ground, and hearing the satisfying thunk of a can being dropped in the chute.

I worked nights then, and was frequently up anyway. So sometimes I'd go out or they'd come in to the two rooms plus bath, and we'd talk, or they'd go wash their faces so they could drive home.

And so it went on, all that summer, and even into the early fall, when school started again, and there were more important things to tend to.

Driving home after night shift, watching the sumac put on her fall coat of purple, gulping coffee to stay awake, I felt the first chill of autumn in the Ozark air.

It was 0810 CDT when I arrived home. Leaving a trail of shoes, socks, uniform, I dropped into bed, and fell into the exhausted sleep that only people who have worked night shift understand. Minutes later, a plane crashed into the first of the Twin Towers. The entire country was being shaken to the core, and I was in dreamland.

The phone ringing at one pm was my wake up call. My father said in a whisper, "You know, our family came in through Ellis Island."

Downstairs, the courtyard was mobbed. We were a different kind of destination that day. The grills were fired up, and covered with trout and roasting ears. I pulled all the peaches I'd canned and folded them into tin foil packets with brown sugar and cinnamon. Those went straight into the coals, and filled the air with a sticky sweet smell.

The Coke machine was restocked twice that day, and that machine held nearly a hundred cans.

We sat out on the stoops, the planters, on blankets by the gardens, or wandered into any of the apartments – no one locked their doors that day – and talked, or comforted babies or watched the horror replay until we just couldn't anymore. Very quickly, we all became very American.

At dusk, people started drifting away. Deb went home with her husband, but Justin and I stayed up, and smoked cigarettes, and watched the midnight sky.

LORAINE FERRARA is originally from New England and now lives in Southern California where she's a member of Laguna Poets.

If you have a skeleton in your closet, take it out and dance with it.

– Carolyn MacKenzie

PAT HUBER

Nympho Neighbors

In 1957, we bought our first house with the help of my parents who gave us our $3,000 down payment on a two bedroom, den, and one-bath home in a nice residential district close to good schools. We were ecstatic with the price of $11,315 and happy to find great and sociable neighbors all around us. Better yet, the monthly payment was $69.00 per month for principal and interest as well as taxes and insurance. Everyone had children around the same age as ours and went to the same school.

The house on our immediate right hand side became a rental but we were fortunate to have primarily very nice neighbors. However, we were surprised when two adult women moved in and shocked when they announced their preferred sexual life. Any heterosexual man would do. There ensued a lot of laughter and admonitions to my husband to be careful while mowing our lawn because if he should trip and fall onto their property, he would be hauled off by his feet into their house and never seen again. I laughed along with the rest of them but soon got used to their coming and goings and for the most part, got used to their coming over to my house to have a cup of coffee and show off their "hunting" clothes. Claire, the mother, worked in a proctologist's office and her daughter went to secretarial school.

My cousin and her third husband, Max Fly, an older bowlegged cowboy, came in from the country to visit me and it was worth the price of admission to see the look on his face when my nympho neighbors popped in to show us their French can-can costumes and gave a brief review of how well they danced. He'd lost his front teeth in a bar fight before they came to visit and was under strict orders not to smile or laugh in front of us. Poor guy just could not stop smiling in spite of the missing teeth.

Several months later, I received an urgent phone call to pick up one of my father's graduate students at LAX in a very short period of time. I quickly called for a babysitter but was only able to get Stevie, another neighbor's son, to sit for me.

Now Stevie was a very good sitter but led a very sheltered life. His mother was a tiger protecting her son from every worldly evil. Imagine my chagrin when Claire walked in as I prepared to leave for the airport. I figured that if I could get rid of her quickly, no harm, no foul would occur but too late, her eyes actually glowed when she saw him. What could I do – I had to pick up Dr. Herrington.

In the early infancy of civilian flight, LAX was housed in wooden barracks at Century and Centinella Boulevards. There were no freeways built as yet and regular street traffic was relatively heavy. However, I was comforted by the thought that if you showed a police officer that you were traveling to or from an airport, they usually waved you on your way without ticket or fine. This, however, did not solve my worries about poor Stevie alone with Claire.

"Would my homeowner's insurance protect me from his mother?"

"Who can I call for help in this emergency?"

I thought that if I could just find a telephone booth, I could call home to check on Stevie.

"Oh, what will I tell my husband?"

"Oh, what will I tell his mother?"

"Oh my God, what will I do? Oh, Oh, Oh – shit!

I finally reached the damned airport, somehow found a parking space, and ran into the barracks, searching for a telephone booth as I dug in my large pocketbook for dimes to make the call. Ding, ding, ding – no answer. Praying, shaking, and sweating, tears filled my eyes. Finally, an answer – it was Claire.

"Where's Stevie?"

"Oh, he's in the bathroom"

"Is he okay?"

"How would I know? I haven't seen him since I got here!"

"Claire, please go home. Stevie is very shy and probably won't come out until you leave. Just leave him alone!"

The phone slammed down to a dial tone.

Still shaking, I picked up Dr. Herrington and raced for home. The trip was a nightmare since I had problems making polite conversation. Upon arriving home, I ran into the house to pay Stevie $5.00 instead of the usual fee of .50 per hour (no matter how many children were involved).

Stevie dashed out of his hiding place and, as I held out the extravagant fee, shouted over his shoulder "No charge, Ma'am – my pleasure" as he headed for the safety of his home.

PAT HUBER writes memoir as well as vignettes based on real life experiences. A resident of Capistrano Beach, she is part of the *Writer's Circle*.

One must avoid ambition in order to write.
Otherwise something else is the goal: some kind of
power beyond the power of language. And the power
of language, it seems to me, is the only kind of power
a writer is entitled to.

— Cynthia Ozick

CATHY TAKECHI

Before The Revolution

Imagine dancing the night away at the Hilton on Pahlavi Street in Tehran.

The seventies were a wonder filled time for a young girl away from her small hometown in Maryland for the first time. Through a volunteer group, I traveled the world to far away places.

When I first arrived in Iran with the American Women's group, our housing arrangements were delayed. We ended up house sitting much of the time in beautiful villas across from the Shah's North Palace where flower gardens blossomed as far as the eye could see.

We worked at an orphanage in Tehran where I assisted with the children's physical therapy. I also participated in fundraisers to raise money that would cover the cost of wheelchairs and surgeries. This was a humbling as well as a gratifying experience for a girl barely out of her teens.

Shiraz, the city of poets, wine and rose gardens, shimmered with beauty and culture. In Hamadan, I wrapped myself in a blanket on the side of a chilly mountain to overlook the fires of Nomad Tribes as wolves howled in the distance.

Chelou kabobs and fresh hot bread from the street ovens were delicious, and the Caspian Sea brought the freshest caviar to tempt my palate.

I found work with a British construction company and felt exotic while learning to belly dance at the Women's Center. I considered myself daring as I smoked a water pipe with the old old men down south.

The Persian people, so warm, welcoming, and floral in thought and deed, became my friends, and I'll never forget them.

Years later, I realize how lucky I was to have been in Tehran before the revolution.

———◆—

CATHY TAKECHI enjoys beautiful sunrises and sunsets while walking the beach with her husband. Some of her favorite learning experiences are meditation, yoga, and Tai Chi. She is currently involved with a writing class to help unleash her imagination and memories.

ALICE SECRIST

Just Like Shirley Temple

I'm five years old. Maw takes me to see all of Shirley Temple's shows. She's only seven years old, but she's a big star out in Hollywood, just like Judy Garland and June Allyson. Everybody goes to see her shows, even old people like our next door neighbor, Mrs. Googe. She's even got a little blue cream pitcher on a shelf in her kitchen with Shirley Temple's face painted on it in white and a little silver spoon with Shirley Temple's face and whole body stamped on the handle.

Shirley Temple is a real good tap dancer, and Maw wants me to learn to dance like Shirley Temple, so she takes me to Hilda Fluegel's beauty shop to make my hair curly like Shirley Temple's. Hilda washes my hair and pours some really bad, smelly stuff on it. Then she rolls up my hair in a lotta, lotta curlers. I want to cry but I don't because Hilda tells me Shirley Temple doesn't cry when she gets her hair curled.

But the next thing Hilda does is hook me and my curlers up to a bunch of electric cords that hang down from a big, round thing high up over my head. That makes my head feel so heavy that I start to bend my neck, but Hilda says I have to keep my head still or my hair might get yanked right out of my head. Then she turns the switch on, and right away my curlers get hot, and my hair starts to smell like it's burning, the way it does when Maw curls it at home with the curling iron that she heats up on our gas stove. So now I do cry and I know Shirley Temple would, too, if somebody did all that to her.

Finally Hilda Fluegel turns the switch off and unhooks all the electric cords. After awhile she pulls out the curlers and combs my hair in fat, Shirley Temple curls. Now I feel like I could fly because my head's not heavy or hot anymore.

After all that, Maw takes me to the dance place. My dance teacher's name is Miss Dentino. She's so pretty, and she can dance almost as good as Shirley Temple can!

Today Paw is taking me for a walk downtown. I'm wearing my white dress. It's got a row of red ribbon across the chest, with square blue buttons sewed on it. I don't know why. They don't button anything. My dress has got little square buttons, round buttons, and funny-shaped buttons printed all over it in red and blue and yellow and orange. I already know all my colors and most of my shapes.

I even know how to read. Uncle Ben taught me how last winter. He was The Fuller Brush Man, but nobody was buying his brushes, so he came and stayed with us until winter was over. I don't blame people for not buying his brushes. Maw brushes my hair with one every morning to get the tangles out, and it pulls so hard that sometimes the whole tangle comes out in the brush. That hurts a lot.

Now Paw and I are in front of Five Points Tavern, and — oh, goody! — we're gonna go inside again today. I'll get to have some pop while Paw drinks his beer. It's real dark in here, but I can see some old men sitting at the bar. There's sawdust on the floor. That's what Paw calls it, but it doesn't look like dust to me. It looks more like the shavings left on our back porch steps after Paw sharpens pencils for me with his pocket knife.

The tavern smells funny. Kinda sweet and a little bit like our cellar at home, but our cellar's got a dirt floor, and this one's made of wood. I'll have to ask Paw about that later.

I'm careful not to step anywhere close to the spittoons. Maw would have a fit if I came home with spittoon juice on my shiny, new white patent leather shoes. I don't know why men chew tobacco, anyway. It tastes so bad they have to keep spitting out the juice. Then they even spit out the tobacco when they're done with it. Sometimes they miss the spittoon and make a mess on the floor. Why don't they just smoke cigarettes like Paw does?

Paw lifts me up onto a barstool cuz it's way too high for me to climb up there. And I'm not near big enough to lean my elbows on the dark, slip'ry bar like the old men do.

Paw gets his beer, and I get a bottle of orange pop. It's so cold it hurts my teeth, and the bubbles make my nose tickle, but it tastes sooo good. I can't have pop at home cuz Maw says it's only for big people like her.

An old man with a black patch on one eye pushes a big ol' bowl of pretzels over in front of me. There's sleeping ladies painted on the outside of the bowl. I want to see if the sleeping ladies go all the way around the bowl because some of them don't have many clothes on. Paw frowns at me and tells me to take some pretzels and give the bowl back to the old man. Yuck! That old guy's got long, dirty fingernails!

The bald-headed old man sitting next to me leans over and says, "Well, little girlie, are you gonna dance fer us again t'day?"

I don't know what to say, so I just lean away from him and back against Paw.

Then some old man with no teeth at all stands up and stares at me. He's got the funniest mouth. It's like a big round "O," and you can see his tongue roll all around in his mouth when he talks.

He says, "Come on, Shirley Temple. Don't be bashful. Get on up there an' dance fer us. I'll give ya a nickel."

Gosh! A nickel! I look at Paw, and he finally nods his head. Then he lifts me up and stands me on the bar. It's just like being on a stage in a real show. Just like Shirley Temple! There's nobody there to play the old piano that stands in the corner, so I just hum a little tune to myself and do some of the new steps I'm learning at Miss Dentino's, like shuffle-ball-change and hop-shuffle-heel-toe heel toe, and some other steps I don't know the names of. When I'm done dancing, I curtsy like Miss Dentino taught us to do.

Then the old men start clapping, and Paw lifts me down and sets me back on my barstool. I get the nickel — and seven pennies, too. I can count the money all by myself: 12 cents! I tie it in a corner of my hankie, like Maw does when she gives me my Sunday School nickel.

A little while later, when Paw and I start to leave, the old men say, "Goodbye,

Shirley Temple" and, "Come back and dance fer us again, Shirley Temple." It makes me feel happy, but Paw says, "Now you remember: don't tell yer Maw about this. She wouldn't like it."

I don't tell her, but she sees me counting out the money and wants to know where it came from. She's frowning, and her eyes are glittery and her face is getting real red, so finally Paw has to tell her.

"What the hell?" she yells. "You let her dance on the bar in the Five Points Tavern fer the whole town to see?"

Then she says a lot more cuss words, but I'm not allowed to say them. (I'm not even spose'ta say "hell.")

Paw says, "The whole town's gonna hear you cussin' a blue streak if you don't calm yerself down."

But, I don't s'pose she hears him cuz she's still yelling to beat the band.

I can't go back to Five Points Tavern anymore, not ever again. That makes me feel sad cuz now nobody will see me dance just like Shirley Temple. Not until we have another dance recital. And that won't be for a long, long time.

ALICE SECRIST participates in several writing critique groups including the Southern California *Word Weavers* and *Saturday Mornings Coffee & Critique*. She is currently concentrating on writing a collection of memoir vignettes.

The Good Samaritans

Steve took another swig from his can of Budweiser. He didn't see the coyote with a black cat clamped between its jaws darting in front of his Lexus. But Mary saw it. The beast sliced through the headlight's beam as it trotted to the other side of the two-lane mountain road.

"Watch out!" she screamed, grabbing the steering wheel, trying to jerk it out of her husband's hands. She saved the animal, but not his beer. Her quick action knocked the can from his hand and into the lap of his rented tuxedo.

"Damn you, Mary!" He glanced down at the beer-soaked trousers while trying to break his wife's grip on the wheel. "Let go!"

But she held fast.

"What the hell are you trying to do? Get us killed?" he yelled.

The battle over the steering wheel cost them dearly. When heading around a long curve, the road took a downhill path. The car picked up momentum and skidded into a guardrail.

The increasing speed snapped the couple to their senses. She let go of the wheel. "Steve!"

He spat out a string of obscenities, mainly directed at her, as he twisted the wheel, trying to keep the car from slamming into the jutting rocks.

"Dear God Almighty, help us!" She braced against the dash and closed her eyes, waiting for impact, preparing to meet the Grim Reaper.

They sideswiped the guardrail. The right headlight shattered; its beam faded. Metal buckled and sparks flew. The steel barrier ended abruptly and the sedan careened off the highway. Strains of metal crunching and groaning played out as the vehicle flew off the road and into a wooded area. Tree trunks and shrubbery scraped against the sides of their vehicle. Steve's face smashed into the steering wheel as the car lurched forward.

Airborne, Mary latched onto the dash and watched tree branches slap the windshield. After crash landing atop a large boulder, the left headlight dimmed. Except for the full moon, darkness. The couple leaned back in their seats and finally exhaled. Blood ran from Steve's forehead and nose.

"Oh my God! You're bleeding!"

Steve pulled a handkerchief from his pocket and wiped his face. Then he pressed the hankie under his nose.

When her trembling hands opened the door, the car teetered. She decided against disembarking when, in the moonlight, she spotted solid ground five feet below their perch. Slowly and carefully, she closed the door.

She fumbled through her handbag on the floorboard and retrieved her cell phone. Its face lit up when she pushed the "on" button. "Out of Range" showed on the screen. Turning it off and on again brought the same result, so she dropped it back into her purse.

"No signal?"

She shook her head.

"Well, that's just great!" He stared through the windshield. "Stuck here…in the middle of God knows where."

Something flew across the windshield.

She screamed. Her stare trailed after the airborne object. "What was that?"

Steve squinted out of the side window. "Looks like a bird or a bat," he answered, reaching for the handle.

"Stop! Don't open it!"

He jerked his hand away. "Why the hell not?"

"Because if we move around too much, we're gonna slide off. We're trapped! We're gonna die!" She held her head in her hands.

"We're not gonna die!" he snapped as blood trickled down into his eyes. He wiped his forehead. "Quit getting so damned hysterical. I can't even think straight with you hollering like that! There's got to be a way outta here."

Gripping the bloody handkerchief, he pounded his fists on the steering wheel. The car swayed. Mary gritted her teeth and grabbed the dash. When the rocking stopped, they leaned back.

She jammed her feet into the open-toed pumps on the floorboard. Then she grabbed her purse and reached for the door handle.

"Where do you think you're going?"

Mary gasped. "Look."

A female mountain lion flanked by four large cubs padded toward them and surrounded their vehicle.

Steve scanned the area until his gaze met theirs. "Holy shit!" He looked as terrified as she felt. "Now what do we do?"

"Pray."

The mother cat stared in at them. Sizing them up? For what? Dinner? Mary closed her eyes and shuddered. A whimper rose and escaped her lips as she instinctively leaned closer to her husband.

Beads of red-tinged sweat dotted Steve's brow as he put his arm around her shoulder, pulling her closer. "I know, Baby. I know."

She clung to her husband and wept. "I never thought we'd die like this."

"Not if I have anything to do about it. Hang on!" He pushed her away and pressed on the horn.

Instead of frightening the animals away, the felines jumped up against the rock, reaching for their car, pawing at it. Even with the windows rolled up tightly, growls reverberated inside the Lexus. The strength of the mountain lions swatting at them rocked the car back and forth. Back and forth. Each jolt more violent than the previous one. Steve's nose banged against the steering wheel.

The momentum knocked them around inside the vehicle. Into each other and against the dash. Once again, his face slammed into the steering wheel, this time knocking him out. His mouth gaped and blood dripped from his chin. She screamed. As the car rocked faster, its undercarriage groaned against the rock. Gas fumes choked her. The largest cat jumped on the hood, salivating as it stared at her through a drool smeared windshield. She shrieked. When the animal's gaze shifted to Steve, it licked its lips. Blood ran down her husband's broken face. Lots of it. She knew what the animal wanted. They were doomed. No match for hungry mountain lions. Feeling helpless and hopeless, she closed her eyes and prepared to die.

The rocking stopped. She peeked through half-closed eyes at the predator still perched on the hood. The cat crouched, looked to his left, and gave out a high pitched scream before jumping off the car. Slowly, Mary opened her eyes completely, in time to see the animals run off. What had frightened them away?

In the distance were men's voices. Muffled. Then sounds of rustling dead brush. Coming closer. She opened her door and shouted, "Hurry! We're over here! My husband's hurt."

A man yelled, "I see them. Over there. On the other side of that boulder."

The footsteps sounded closer now. Two male figures sprinted toward the car. Tall men wearing black clothes and heavy boots.

"Thank God, you found us," she sobbed.

The dark-haired one shimmied up the rock and held her door open. A handsome face. Funny how she noticed that. "Hold on, Ma'am. Are you okay?"

"I am," she answered, looking at Steve. "But my husband. I think he's unconscious."

The second man, a blond, crawled up the other side of the boulder and eyeballed Steve. "I can see that. Don't worry, we'll take care of him." Without faltering, he kept the car still and pulled open the driver's door. He moved Steve's head from side to side.

"What's your name, Ma'am?" He gently leaned Steve's head back onto the headrest, holding it in place.

"Mary," she answered, her eyes focused on her husband. "Is he okay?"

"He's lost a lot of blood."

"Can you save him?"

"He's...still...bleeding," he answered, leaning over him, nearly covering his body.

The car rocked slightly, then stabilized. Relief flooded over her. Help was here. She sighed. They were in capable hands. "Thank you...thank you. How can we ever repay you for rescuing us."

The dark-haired man answered, "Don't worry, Ma'am. This is payment enough."

"But I want to pay you. Please. It's the least I can do. How much? Name your price," she prattled as she reached for her purse.

"He's losing a lot of blood," the blonde man groaned.

The dark-haired man's fingers grazed her cheek. "Mary?" he whispered.

She bolted up and gulped. Her heart pounded. He had her attention.

"Put your purse away. I don't want your money. But a drink will suffice." He leaned in and pushed her hair away from her neck. "If you don't mind, I'd much rather have a Bloody Mary."

JOYCE WARD has tried her hand at screenplays and fiction. Published in Interstices, the Orange County Anthology, she is a member of several critique groups including the *Writer's Circle and Saturday Mornings Coffee & Critique*. She's currently working on a vampire novel set in San Juan Capistrano.

Black and White

As a little white girl and extremely shy, I thought elementary school would be like a big library. With two older brothers and one older sister, I learned to weigh my words to avoid hand-to-hand combat. That meant I didn't talk very much, answer questions, or interrupt their conversations.

School brought even more intimidation for someone so shy. Being meek, I was cast as Mary in the Nativity scene.

The kids teased me, pulled my hair and yelled things like, "Hey, stupid, can't you talk?"

One day on the playground, a boy grabbed a handful of sand and threw it at my face. "Say something, runt!"

Suddenly Margie stepped into the fray. A big girl from the black orphanage, she'd been my friend ever since the day we sat abandoned on a bench and traded sandwiches. Without a hesitation, Margie shoved the bully aside and shouted. "Stop hurting my little Jeanie!"

She pulled me to the side of her tall body where I felt saved. Taking a wide stance, hands on her hips, she glared at the boy with steely black eyes and said, "Don't mess with me."

The bully took one look at my Margie and ran off. All the kids laughed and called him a sissy. Gratitude filled me to the brim.

A few days later, I climbed onto the city bus and, spotting Margie at the back, ran eagerly to sit beside her.

The bus suddenly screeched to a stop in the middle of the block.

Startled, chatter along the aisle ceased as the bearded, heavyset driver stood up with a scowl and lumbered to the rear of the bus. He grabbed me by the arm and yanked me out of the seat and brought me to my feet. I looked at Margie but her eyes gazed at the bus driver's shoes. Too shy to protest, I allowed the man to nudge me past all the staring eyes to the front of the bus.

Being a good, if timid, little girl, no one scolded me at school, and I'd never gotten into trouble on the bus.

The driver shook a finger in my face and bellowed, "*She* knows her place. Why don't you know *yours?*"

It seemed he was talking about Margie, and I had no idea I had a special place.

Soldiers were fighting in Europe and fleets were crossing the Pacific in defense of freedom, but we all had our precise places on the American homefront. Even at school, everyone stayed with a group.

Through my friend Margie from the black orphanage, I learned about segregation. That was long ago but even then I thought, "Someone's wrong here, and I don't think it's me."

CATHERINE FISHBERG has participated in Reader's Theater, acted at the Moulton Playhouse, and been on stage at the Pageant of the Masters. She enjoys reading, writing, and journaling.

ANNIE MOOSE

Wonder Years

I just got word that one of the most tragic figures from my childhood has died at the age of 49. He was tragic because his life, from very early on, was characterized by violence, drugs, and crime. He plain and simply wasted his life. But he wasn't underprivileged, or, as far as I know, from a broken or particularly unhappy home. If you were to ask people who knew him what his problem was, most would say that he was just plain bad. It's tempting to believe that something must have been amiss in his family for him to have turned out so badly, but a surprising number of kids I grew up with had similar stories. Ronny was one of the worst, to be sure, but he was just one of a long list of kids in my charming tree-lined neighborhood who went wrong at a very early age.

This morning I was thinking about Ronny and the other kids I grew up with, and I began to wonder how differently we might all have turned out if our parents had had the same kid-centric approach to parenting that is prevalent today. During my Wonder Years—which were the sixties and early seventies—there were no soccer moms. There were stay home moms aplenty, but in those days family life was not centered around kids' activities and concerns. There was no litany of lessons and extracurricular activities, no homework or major school projects to speak of, and no special testing for learning disabilities or different cognitive styles. When we weren't in school, we were mostly thrown outdoors and told to come back at dinnertime. There was the odd kid on a swim team or in Little League, and girls sometimes had ballet or piano lessons once a week, but, for the most part, we were left to our own devices. For many of us this meant smoking in the schoolyard, hanging out at unsupervised homes, and generally running wild. By the age of twelve, many kids like Ronny were already smoking pot, drinking, and experimenting with drugs. Mostly it was the kids with older brothers and sisters who began so young. If our senior siblings were taking drugs in high school, we took them in junior high—or, in some cases, in fifth or sixth grade.

I was a good student and basically a good kid, but even I was smoking cigarettes pretty seriously by thirteen. Like most children in those years, I was born into an atmosphere of smoke. Now my parents are ashamed to recall their behavior, but they used to smoke in the car with the windows rolled up, and they thought nothing of smoking in a house filled with kids. In my family, we sometimes joke about how my mom smoked while breast feeding. To their credit, both my parents quit smoking by the time I was in the second grade, but I'm convinced that by then I was already addicted to nicotine, or at least predestined to smoke, because I was always attracted to smoking. I can remember craving cigarettes as far back as grammar school, and lots of kids were like that. We were programmed to smoke by our parents, and, unfortunately, smoking put us in a mindset that led to other things.

For me and others like me, smoking cigarettes was a natural lead-in to smoking pot. By age fourteen, I'd already quit marijuana, which made me hallucinate, and caused other sensations that really scared me. I remember trying to eat dinner one night and not being able to distinguish my tongue from the food I was chewing, all the while trying to appear normal to my parents. It makes me cringe to recall this, but I also remember playing a "game" that involved taking a hit of marijuana, then hyperventilating for the purpose of deliberately passing out. Now, of course, I know that this can cause serious brain damage — sometimes even death — but then I was completely clueless. We were all clueless, particularly our parents, who knew nothing of the drugs that were increasingly part of our world.

It was the epicenter of the drug era, and many kids who started experimenting with drugs did *not* quit by fourteen. They kept going, and progressed to harder and more dangerous substances. I remember kids in my junior high school taking *reds, yellows, beans, mushrooms, acid, mescaline, heroin, cocaine…*. Many left school in ambulances. The person who first introduced me to marijuana died of a drug overdose when she was eighteen. She was the mellowest of a group of kids who used to terrorize anyone who came near their short street, which we called "Bully Boulevard."

A surprising number of bullies lived within close radius of my house, and I remember very few instances in which parents became involved in the "disturbances" that occurred when one of these predators decided to have some fun. One of the most despised and notorious bullies of all lived at the end of my street. My most memorable experience with him occurred when I was about ten or eleven. I had climbed up on my best friend's roof and was discovered there by this bully, who proceeded to pelt me with dirt clods. *Big, rock-hard dirt clods.* I was eventually rescued by a neighbor who heard me screaming, but not before I was pretty seriously traumatized. And I was *very* lucky to have been saved, because this boy was not the type to show mercy. He once forced open the eyes of a litter of kittens, or so it was told. This boy was so feared and reviled in our neighborhood that even the parents booed him at his high school graduation. And he was just one of the unsavory characters on my block. Another teenage malcontent used to dangle his penis out his second story window and yell obscenities to girls walking home from school. My beautiful neighborhood might have looked like *Leave it to Beaver*, but the reality was much different.

My parents still live in that neighborhood, but I don't think such things go on anymore. Nowadays, "problem" kids are more likely to be identified as learning disabled, or in need of special programs, and parents are much more in tune with their kids' activities and whereabouts. And bullies are certainly much less tolerated. When I was in junior high school, students brought knives, pins, and all kinds of scary implements to school. And they used them! These days, you're suspended if you're caught with so much as a butter knife in your lunch pail. Which is not to say that there are no problems. I think the pendulum has probably swung too far the other way. Now, half the kids are on Ritalin, and many are stressed from an overload of activities and homework. But we baby boomers *have* learned a lot from our parents' mistakes. We know about drugs and the dangers of too little supervision — because we lived it.

As for Ronny, I can't help wondering how he might have turned out if his parents and teachers had paid more attention. Maybe he'd have loved soccer, or been a star gymnast. Maybe he'd have been diagnosed as dyslexic and gotten some help. Who knows, maybe he *was* just plain bad. But contemplating his death, and his sad, wasted life, I'd like to think that perhaps it wasn't all his fault. He may simply have been a casualty of a dangerous time to be a kid. And it really *was* a dangerous time to be a kid. At least it was in *my* picture-book neighborhood.

ANNE MOOSE is a technical writer, author of Berkeley USA, and editor of several books, including Proteus Rising, by Peter Dingus, and Dakota Diaspora: Memoirs of a Jewish Homesteader, by Sophie Trupin. Her writing has been published in Interstices, the Orange County Anthology. She's currently working on short pieces based on her life.

She Writes

Encore

Barbie Girl

It starts out as a normal enough day, the day I get the fateful call – the call to be Barbie. On the phone with the children's birthday party agency that assigns me the parties, I try to feign the appropriate excitement, but I can feel my panic building as the agent tells me that there's no costume, wig, or props to pick up before the party.

He says, "That's the great part about this gig – just go as you are. You are still a blonde, right? Oh, and wear something 'Barbie-ish.' You're perfect for this. You'll be great."

I get off the phone and my initial worry begins to blossom into a full-blown panic attack. My eye is twitching uncontrollably. Other than that, I am numb. Why did I say yes? I'm sure they just couldn't find anyone else to do this party so they had to resort to me.

What have I gotten myself into? Sure, thanks to L'Oreal, I do, indeed, have long blonde hair, but while Barbie's is silky, straight and shiny, mine is wavy, thick and full of split ends. But my hair insecurities are only the beginning. My nose is too big, my smile is not white enough, my chest is too small and my hips are too big. I am so imperfect. Barbie is an icon for God's sake.

As I don't have the money, the time or, most importantly, the inclination, for radical plastic surgery, I have no idea how I will pull this off. I start worrying that I have Barbie's figure only if you thought of her standing on her head. It's just like one of the old SAT analogies, "Barbie's Hips are to Debby's Chest as Debby's Hips are to Barbie's Bust."

I come back out of my disassociative state of panic. I get some water, sit down, and try to be rational. I've played Pocahontas without a Native American background; I've played The Little Mermaid without really having a fish tail. Hell, I played Barney and I'm not a purple dinosaur. Then, it dawns on me. Barbie wears no recognizably distinct costume.

When I'm wearing Jasmine's wig and satiny teal harem pants, it doesn't seem to matter to my audience that my eyes aren't dark brown, or that they don't take up roughly a third of my face like the cartoon girl's. Unfortunately, part of Barbie's appeal is that she wears many different outfits and has marvelously style-able hair. She's a chameleon. That's what little girls and gay men love the most about her.

I begin to doodle on a piece of paper I have on the table by the phone. The only defining characteristic of Barbie that I can come up with is that she is undeniably, impossibly perfect. How can I be Barbie? The next two days I eat only salads and apply two different conditioning treatments to my hair.

Of course, all of this worry causes a beauty of a pimple to erupt in the middle of my left cheek the morning of the dreaded party day. Now I am going to be "Pizza Face Barbie." Great. After attempting to smother the angry red head of my new zit with layers of blemish concealer, I strap myself into a padded bra, a borrowed pink mini-dress and a pair of white go-go boots with four-inch heels. I put on a brave face. I also brush my teeth twice and put on my brightest red lipstick. As I stand in front of the door to the party house, I try not to let myself dwell on the many ways I don't measure up to Barbie. I need the money. I need the job.

I walk up to the house of the birthday party, festively decorated with balloons tied to the mailbox by the street, some with Barbie's picture on them, taunting me. I try to push all of this from my mind. Barbie would be thinking about sunny beach parties and shopping for new clothes with Midge.

The five-year-old Birthday Girl answers the door herself and eyes me suspiciously from head to toe. "Cathy?" I ask and she nods. I try not to gulp audibly.

"Yes?" She answers simply, politely even; maybe this won't be too hard. She seems sweet.

"I am Barbie." Silence.

Then Cathy puts her hands on her hips. "You're not!"

"Sure I am," I start, trying not to let my dismay show. "I just came from my Malibu Dream House where I was playing with my sister, Skipper!" Cathy doesn't look convinced, so I keep babbling. "Well, I'd better come in now so we can get this great birthday party started because I have to meet my boyfriend Ken for a big date later in my Pink Convertible Corvette.... " I am acutely aware of my own dirty Subaru lurking in the only parking spot I could find, almost directly across the street. Hopefully she did not see me sneak out of the passenger side of it five minutes ago. I tried to keep low when I did.

"You're NOT Barbie," she says, a bit more forcefully now, shaking her head emphatically. I want to give up. I can't take this anymore. Everything in me is screaming not to ask the next, logical, question. But I can't think of anything else to do.

"Why do you think that I'm not Barbie?" I brace myself. Children can be very cruel. I try to smile as big and as dazzling a smile as I can, hoping to blind her.

She looks confused, and sizes me up again before she answers. "You're not Barbie, because Barbie is only THIS BIG!" She holds out her hands to approximate Barbie's undeniable twelve-inch height. In my frenzy of insecurity, the most obvious difference between the doll and myself had never occurred to me. Giddy relief washes over me.

"Oh right, I see!" I try not to giggle. I hear myself explain to her that I am the real Barbie, the human Barbie, on whom the doll had been based.

Breaking into an excited grin, Cathy grabs my hand, "Oh! The real Barbie! I get it! Wow."

She leads me around the party, proudly introducing me to her friends as the "Real Barbie." I feel so great. I even eat a piece of the birthday cake when it is offered to me. I am the Real Barbie today so it is impossible for me to get fat. Unfortunately, I have to leave after an hour and a half, as I do have that previously arranged date with Ken.

When I get to my car and realize that it has not changed into a pink convertible, I keep walking. I want to stay Barbie for just a few more minutes before I have to double-back and sneak into that old rundown Subaru.

— DEBBY DODDS

When I'm not writing, I can't make sense of anything.
I feel the need to make some sense and find some order,
and writing fiction is the only way I've found that seems
to begin to do that. Even if the story or the novel ends up
saying there is no sense and there is no order, at least I've
made that much of an attempt.

— Alice McDermott

Cross Purposes

After more than 20 years together
you've never come to a poetry reading,
competition or open mike night.
That's not to say
you haven't heard me
read aloud as I pound
the keyboard tweaking the sound,
massaging the metaphor,
birthing the poem.
You never react to the excitement
and pride I feel inside
when I know I've just produced
a slamming piece.

If I ask you to listen,
you react like a cat
dangling over a vat of water
squirming,
searching for any excuse
to be anywhere else.
And yes, I persist,
in the face of your resistance
to draw you into my world
striving to share a piece of my soul
because in my mind, in my heart
that's what married people do
to stay connected.

You never truly listen.
You fidget and twitch
with glassy eyes
that scream their disinterest.
And when I finish

it's as if my words
had been swallowed by a black hole
or never spoken.
Your only comment is how
you had to change the specs
from American to Metric today
and how the manufacturing line
is just too stupid to get it.

I recognize that poetry isn't your thing.
I completely understand
you'd rather be watching the Science channel
or calculating the solution
to a mathematical equation
than to listen to one of my poems.
But I yearn for your support,
even if it's feigned interest.
Please, just show me the respect
I give you
because in my mind, in my heart
that's what married people do
to stay connected.

❖

Surreal

As if some Hollywood director
had called *It's a wrap*,
the clapboard falls on the final scene.
Robotic submersibles surfaced and stowed,
no longer need to illuminate
twisted steel girders,
blown drill heads and bowed pipes -
the skeletal remains of Deep Water Horizon
strewn across the gulf floor.

Flanked by self-satisfied officials
before a room of microphone booms,
clicking cameras and network talking heads,
today's script highlights celebration,
holds no hint of conflict, no discussion
of missed deadlines and maintenance delayed,
of bypassed shut-off valves
or fire sirens silenced by too many false alarms,
always the cheap fix sacrificed for the bottom line.

No, today the villain is vanquished,
the hero declares,
crammed with concrete like
a rogue hitman fitted
with a cement overcoat.
Today, in this stereo-typical Happy Ending
like the Wicked Witch of the West,
The well is not only merely dead,
it's really most sincerely dead.

But wait,
this is Hollywood baby
there is always a sequel.

❖

The Patient

I am the spinal fusion
in 419-bed-A.
I'm the clear liquid diet,
the almost empty IV *banana bag*
the morphine PCA -
just another checkmark
in the Medication Log,
another *encouraged ambulation*
chart notation.

I'm the "I'll get your nurse"
bathroom request filled
thirty minutes too late.
Eyes refuse to meet eyes
as you roll me like an inert log,
strip the sheets,
diaper my backside,
then chastise me
to call
sooner
next time.

I'm just the patient
in room 419-bed-A.
I have no name.

— Shayla Rosofsky

The Woman in the Shocking Pink Hat

Jen's voice comes in a rush when I answer my cell. "What's the matter with Mom?" she gasps. "Honestly, Kate, you ought to call her more often."

Like a defendant, I slump in my chair. "Look, Jen, I have a life, sort of, and I've been really busy lately."

Sounds lame, even to me. I know what she thinks.

"We're *all* busy," she says. "You can fly down to see her in an hour. I have to go across the entire country." As usual, there's an edge to her voice. Jen lives the good life in New York with a proper husband and two children while I, still single, slog through legal papers in San Francisco. "Mom just called," she says. "We have a *crisis*."

Alerted, I straighten into the family ramrod. "Is she all right?"

"Well, for your information, she's not having Thanksgiving this year."

"Thanksgiving? Already?" I glance at the wall calendar cluttered with depositions, court appearances, and billable hours. "Look, Jen, can't we live without Mom's turkey for once?"

"But we *always* have Thanksgiving with Mom. Even last year we crammed into that tiny apartment she rented. Remember how we had to juggle plates on our knees and kept knocking over glasses? Quite a come-down for us all."

"Divorce changes everything," I say.

"You don't understand how serious this is, Kate. Our mother's been – well, doing odd things lately."

"Like what?"

"Dumpster diving."

My head throbs. "You mean she's going through people's trash?"

"Exactly."

"Trash with leftover pizza and old broken furniture?"

"You've got to take her in."

"Me? Why me?" Scenes of my dismal flat flash through my mind. Jen doesn't realize I'm a slob. She has all the ammunition – a husband, children, and distance. My mouth marches ahead of my common sense without any help from me. "I suppose she can come visit, sleep on the futon for a couple of nights." I roll my thumb against my right temple. "I think she's allergic to cats though, and I still have Precious and – what exactly do you mean by 'dumpster diving'?"

"If she hadn't been dumpster diving, she would never have found the hat."

"What hat?"

"Honestly, Kate, if you'd call her once in awhile, you'd know all about the pink hat. You wouldn't have to hear it from me."

An arrow of guilt shoots through my brain. All four lines on my office phone signal incoming calls. "I'm really busy, Jen. If Mom doesn't want to cook a turkey this year, why don't we take her to a nice restaurant? You can come out with the family and Mom can fly up from Orange County. I'll make reservations."

She sighs. "Listen, Kate, you don't get it." Her words wobble like a Thanksgiving Jell-O mold. Then she takes a deep breath and says, "Mom's taking herself on the *road*! Call her, *now*, on her cell."

"Her cell?" I snatch the half empty bottle of Advil from a desk drawer cluttered with abandoned business cards picked up in bars. "Mom doesn't have a cell."

"She does now. Guess where she found it. Top of the line, too."

I try to picture my ordinary, run-of-the-mill, rather elderly mother picking up hats, mildewed coats, and discarded electronics out of garbage containers.

I add Mom's cell number to my contact list under the name "Mom."

"Bye, Jen. I've got to work." It's no lie. "We'll figure it out. Later."

She ends the call before I get a chance. She won at Scrabble, too, and finished algebra homework faster and had more boyfriends. Even though she has a law degree, she stays home to make brownies with her girls.

I've always idolized my sister, but she expects too much of me. Mom needs a life, but not mine. What I need is a different job, a new boyfriend, a bigger apartment, and it wouldn't hurt my review any to have more billable hours.

A knock on the door brings the *Chronicle* with caffeine. My secretary adds files to the towering stack on my desk. I spin in my chair to acknowledge the Golden Gate out my window. It gleams orange over the gray sea. The French Roast alleviates the sinus pressure but increases my anxiety. Has it been nearly a year since we had Mom's overcooked turkey, too-sweet cranberry sauce, and that inescapable string bean casserole? I wonder if Dad might be up for Thanksgiving. He's still in the big OC with possession of the dining room table, crystal, and Noritake China.

As I swivel around, newspapers spill to the floor. I reach for a section of the *Chronicle*, and Mom, wearing a broad-brimmed hat, smiles at me from the back page. The hat, an electric pink, is the only color on a full-page B&W advertisement. That hat is the most vivid pink I've ever seen, huge, and a floppy fake cherry-red rose decorates the wide band. Across the ad in white font as dignified as a Streisand program are the words: *On Tour! One Night Only. The Woman in the Shocking Pink Hat.*

"What the hell?" Attempting to get a closer look, I spill coffee across my mother's face. "Damn!" All but the vivid hat and a phone number are obliterated. I compare the number to the latest addition on my cell and then press "send" without even thinking.

One ring. Two. Three. Then: "The Woman in the Shocking Pink Hat."

The words lilt; she sounds more like my sister than herself.

"Mom?"

"Thank you for calling." Her recorded voice scoops me up and sweeps me in. "I'm on tour at the moment but look forward to talking to you soon. Carpe Diem."

Stunned, I leave some sort of message, something like, "Hey, uh, Mom, it's your wayward youngest about Thanksgiving. Give me a ring."

The idea of Mom with a cell phone is baffling enough. She's always the last to know, the one who never changes, and how she ever figured out voicemail is beyond me. I thought I could rely on my same old, Thanksgiving-hosting, cranberry-sauce-making, regular sort of mother. I don't know this confident sounding woman at all.

I want to call Jen. Is this some kind of joke? Revenge for not keeping in touch with the family the way Jen thinks I should? I decide to lose myself in work.

Plucking a personal injury file from the stack, I sort correspondence three inches thick. I don't like medical malpractice any better than personal injury or bankruptcy. The truth is I don't like law at all and only went into it because of Dad and Jen. Of course, Jen married a lawyer and her student loans are paid off. Mine aren't.

When my cell rings, it flashes "Mom" on the screen. It's no joke. It's her, only newer and better. "Sweetheart!" She speaks in a rush as if dashing from one appointment to another. "Got your voicemail. Delighted to hear from you."

"Sorry I haven't been in touch lately."

"Me, too. I'm so busy these days. You sound worn out, Dear. Are you working too hard? I have so much to tell you. Are you at the office?"

"Let me block my calls." I press buttons on my desk phone to place incoming billable hours into a holding pattern. I've never in my whole life stopped doing whatever I'm doing for her. "Jen's worried about you, Mom. What's this about not having Thanksgiving?"

"Oh, no time for all that, Dear. It's just that I've let my apartment go and I have other plans and, to tell you the truth, I've never felt so free."

"Where are you living?"

"Oh, nowhere in particular, Dear."

"Jen says you're digging through trash."

"And why not? It's going to waste otherwise. Rich people throw perfectly good things away: Dolce & Gabbana, Louis Vuitton. You just have to know where and when to look. I've picked up some really nice things and given them to the women's shelter."

"That was generous." I sound bitter even to myself.

"Oh, I've saved an item or two for you and Jen."

I remember Mom walking precincts when Dad ran for the judgeship and how she sold all those boxes of Girl Scout cookies the troop dumped on our doorstep. Mom organized sleepovers at the zoo for needy children, convinced a dozen neighbors to install solar panels on Earth Day, and she always had Thanksgiving.

"And the hat?" I ask.

"You know about the hat? Changed my life. The minute I plopped it on my head, I started thinking of infinite possibilities. Actually, all any woman needs is a really good hat. I told that to the young man doing my YouTube video. He got such a kick out of it that he put me on FaceBook and all those twittery places, social networking it's called, and I have so many friends now that I can't keep track – but I suppose you know about all that, Dear."

"You have a computer now?" I say in disbelief.

"Several. Need a laptop? It's so hard to keep up to date these days. People discard perfectly good equipment all the time. I donated fifty working sets to your old elementary school and they set up a computer lab."

"Maybe you should come stay with me awhile," I suggest.

"I have a publisher. Did I tell you? Nice advance, too. Life is so much easier these days, don't you think? They're coming up with a phone that allows you to talk with someone in any language. Amazing. Connects us, you see. No one speaks the same language anymore. I don't know how many times I told your father –"

"You're speaking to Dad?"

"All the time." She laughs. "Look, I landed in San Francisco a couple of hours ago. I was about to call when you rang."

"You're here?"

"Isn't it wonderful? I can't believe how this shocking pink hat thing has taken off. Are you coming to my performance tonight? Palace of Fine Arts?"

***

My sister answers her cell on the first ring. "Did you call Mom?" she asks.

"I not only talked to her, I went to her performance," I say. "Compelling, Jen. I was completely blown away. I woke up today knowing I was a different person."

She chokes or maybe coughs. I hear the clatter of dishes. "Oh, my God! You mean, people actually come to see Mom in a big hat?"

"It's an exquisite hat."

"Bet no one showed up. Right?"

"Standing room only."

"You're not serious. She doesn't have one shred of talent. I ought to know. I inherited her genes. What does she actually *do?*"

"She talks."

"About what?" she asks.

"She's different, Jen. It's a life changing experience to see her in that pink hat."

"She's lost it, Kate. And maybe you have, too. We've got to put her somewhere." I hear the tapping of a pencil against her granite counter. "I can't have her here, not in the same kitchen. Do I introduce her to friends as the lady in the pink hat?"

"The hat's only a symbol."

"Of what, for God's sake?"

"Well, I don't know. Empowerment, I guess. Authenticity. Mom's the real deal."

"People *actually* pay money to see Mom wearing a hat?"

"No one pays. It's free. Avoids bad reviews."

"You've got to be kidding. She gets reviews?"

I pick up the morning paper. "Here's the *Chronicle*. Listen to this: 'The Woman in the Shocking Pink Hat combines intoxicating eccentricity with good common sense to regale anyone eager to discover what's under her hat and on her mind.'" I pause, but Jen's speechless. A feeling of elation keeps me smiling even though I have plenty to do. I select the *Guardian*. "Here's another: 'There's something fabulous about her blatant sarcasm. Her cynicism rings true. Audiences adore her badness. The Woman in the Shocking Pink Hat commands the stage with consummate skill.'"

I hear Jen's intake of breath through phone static as I pull files from my briefcase and pile them atop the desk. How light I feel. It's like floating or being in love.

"I can't believe this," she gasps.

"She's writing a book," I say.

"What about?"

"About choosing to be happy, about dumpster diving, of course, about being true to yourself and following your dreams."

"No one will read it."

"She's pre-sold thousands of copies already. It'll be on eBook and Kindle soon. And a producer –"

"A producer? You mustn't encourage her, Kate."

"If Mom can do it, why can't I?"

"What do you mean?"

"I handed in my resignation this morning. Effective immediately. I've already sublet my flat to someone who will take care of the cat. Mom wants me to edit the book, set up the salons, and head up the recycling centers."

"What about Dad?" Jen asks. "Maybe he'll do us a favor and take her back."

"Look, Jen, I've got to catch BART, get on a plane, and stop by the thrift store for a really good hat."

"What about Thanksgiving?"

"Problem solved," I say. "Mom's booked on Broadway at the Winter Garden and is preparing a universal gratitude feast afterwards."

"What the hell's that?"

"Beans and rice. Why don't you come?"

"But I'm talking about *Thanksgiving*, Kate."

"So am I," I say. "So am I."

– MARYANN EASLEY

The patriarchal world – meaning the white man, basically
– deals with knots by just cutting through them, which
never teaches you anything. Whereas untying a knot
teaches you because you really have to work at it.

– Alice Walker

The Box of Crayons

It was the last day of school before Christmas break, and our holiday party was in full swing. The room was bustling with excitement, as the aromas and sounds of the season permeated the air and told us that Christmas was near.

Mrs. Sweet, my kindergarten teacher, was busy scurrying about the room, and handing out the gifts we had all brought for our holiday gift exchange. I squirmed impatiently in my chair as I waited for her to make her way across the room to Table Three. I could hear the table's sturdy oak frame creak and groan beneath my weight as I adjusted my position and waited.

"Look what I got!" I heard Angela yell from across the room as she held up a jump rope and Jack set.

"I got a car!" Jeff called out, as several boys gathered around him and jockeyed for position to get a closer look. I wondered who would be the lucky recipient of the grey stuffed elephant I had brought to exchange.

I twisted around in my chair and was able to make out the top of Mrs. Sweet's dark hair bobbing up and down as she navigated her way through the sea of students toward our table.

"Mrs. Sweet is coming!" Steven shrieked.

"Here you go. And, here *you* go," she muttered as she made her way around the table setting a wrapped gift on the table in front of each of us.

I stared at the rectangular shaped box in front of me while the rest of my tablemates tore into their packages. I was careful to not make any unnecessary tears in the bright red and white peppermint striped paper. I opened one end at a time the way my mother had taught me. Mom was adamant about recycling most everything, and wrapping paper was no exception.

As I peeled away the last bit of paper I could see that it was a box of crayons. I ran my fingers over its smooth surface and admired the uniform rows of colors that resembled little toy soldiers standing at attention. This was no ordinary box of crayons. It was the biggest box of crayons I had ever laid eyes on.

The oversized box boasted a variety of seventy-two colors. Included, were all sorts of new and exciting hues like copper, sky blue, and Indian red. There were even some colors that I had never heard of before, like tangerine, and magenta. I liked the sound of them, and the way the names rolled off my tongue when I tried to pronounce them.

On the back of the box were two built-in sharpeners, essential tools for only the most serious of artists. I was thrilled. And then, without warning, my moment of bliss was interrupted when I heard the voice.

"Those are mine! *I* brought that gift!" The high-pitched declaration came from across the table. I raised my head and peered over the rims of my brown tortoise shell glasses, nudging them up onto the bridge of my nose as I looked in the direction the voice had came from.

"Those are mine! *I* brought that gift!" The voice came again. Only this time it was louder, and laced with more than just a hint of impatience.

I glanced down at the discarded wrapping paper and the Holly Hobby Colorforms that sat on the table in front of her. It was clear that she had misunderstood the concept of gift "exchange." She thought that the gift she had brought to exchange belonged to her. And, she wanted my crayons.

I sat in silence and diverted my glance back to the box of crayons, trying with earnest to avoid her piercing stare. She stretched her arms out in front of her, as she leaned across the table toward me.

"Give them to me," she said.

I scanned the room, desperate for some assistance. I tried to call out to Mrs. Sweet as she hurried past, but she didn't notice as my voice had become trapped in my throat and would not rise above a whisper.

I looked at the girl with her gaze fixed on me and her arms outstretched in entitlement, and then back to the box of crayons. I felt powerless and afraid. With reluctance, I slowly pushed the box across the table and into the girl's impatient hands. She snatched them up in haste, and my heart sank.

I sat in silence, unable to talk and unable to move. I looked around the room at the rest of my classmates intoxicated with laughter and excitement as they talked and shared amongst themselves. My throat grew tight and ached as I felt the lump inside it begin to grow. It took all of my strength to keep the tears that were welling up in my eyes from spilling down my cheeks. I waited for what seemed like an eternity for the school bell to ring. At last it sounded, and in an instant the room was a flurry of activity as children rushed to gather their belongings and scurried out into the schoolyard.

The crisp winter air burned my cheeks as I ran the short distance home to my grandmother's house. I burst through the front door, out of breath and hysterical.

"What's the matter?" Grandma demanded, as she came rushing in from the kitchen. I collapsed into her strong arms. My sobs were muffled as I buried my face in her blouse and hugged her tight around the waist.

"I didn't get a gift! I didn't get a gift! I was the only one in the whole class who didn't get a gift!" I whispered in between sobs. She seemed confused at first but once I had calmed down and explained in detail what had happened, she nodded her head with understanding.

"Wait here," she said and then disappeared into her bedroom. She emerged a few moments later carrying a small white box.

"Here is your gift," she said as she placed the box in my outstretched hand.

Inside the box was a bottle of perfume designed in the shape of a Christmas stocking. The lid resembled a tiny red jingle bell. It sparkled with radiance as the light reflected off its shiny surface. It was likely one of her free gifts with purchase from her latest Avon order. I marveled at being the recipient of such a sophisticated gift and smiled.

"Thank you, Grandma," I told her. "I love it."

"You're welcome, Honey," she said as she leaned down and kissed the top of my head. Her gift of love had somehow helped to heal the pain of my five-year-old broken heart. And for that moment, the box of crayons was nothing but a distant memory.

Years later, when I was a freshman in college, I was given a creative writing assignment in one of my classes. I chose to tell my story about the box of crayons. When our papers were returned to us, my professor asked me to share my story aloud to the rest of the class. My emotions took me by surprise as I felt that familiar lump begin to form in the back of my throat, making it difficult to speak.

"Not now!" I thought as I struggled to compose myself. At once I recalled the tremendous loss and disappointment I had felt that day in kindergarten. My vision began to blur as tears welled up in my eyes. I laughed aloud, in an attempt to detract from my obvious emotion. I muddled through the reading in a haze and then quickly took my seat.

The following week I was outside the student union when one of my classmates, George, motioned for me to come over. I knew George from class, but we had never socialized outside of that.

"Hey, do you have a minute?" he asked. "I have something for you in my car." I had no idea what to expect as we walked to his car parked in the nearby student lot.

"What is it?" I asked feeling a little uncomfortable.

"Just wait, you'll see," he said. When we arrived at his car, he reached into the back seat and pulled out something. He tried to keep it sheltered behind his back and out of my direct view.

"I felt really bad for you when you were reading your paper out loud in class last week," he explained. "I know those tears in your eyes weren't just from laughing. So, here, these are for you."

It was a box of crayons, just like the one from my kindergarten gift exchange. A red floppy bow had been tied neatly around it.

"George, thank you," I said. "I can't believe you did this."

"No problem," he said. We stood there in awkward silence for a few moments, neither of us sure what to say next.

"Well, I have to get to class," I said. "I guess I'll see you on Thursday."

"Yeah, see you on Thursday," he said. I turned and made my way back in the direction of campus, smiling and with my box of crayons clutched tight against my chest.

I didn't end up marrying George. I will, however, always hold a special place for him in the young heart he was so instrumental in helping to heal.

There is an old cliché about how big gifts often come disguised in small packages. I'm a believer. And in my case, they sometimes come disguised as a simple box of crayons.

— MICHELE RUVALCABA

You only learn to be a better writer by actually writing.

— Doris Lessing.

The m&m's

The Noisy Pelican is a seaside bar that serves tortillas and beans, and three-buck lager until seven p.m., every night of the week. I go there to eat and haven't cooked since Louie walked out on me last year. My waistline has spread from too many tortillas, with a roll of fat that I reach for and grip nice and tight when I'm feeling lonesome.

Louie used to take me out for steaks with all the trimmings and say wonderful things to me. When he touched me he said my skin felt like white velvet. He loved my red hair and would nestle his nose deep into it, and then say he could smell the family we would make together. When I sit at home alone, I wonder whose hair he's smelling now – so I stay mostly at the bar.

Natalie would talk about Louie with me. She and I were best friends since the third grade and talked about everything. We always said that life's a game, like Wheel of Fortune. Six months ago, on her thirty-second birthday, Natalie spun the wheel, landed on lose your turn and was out of the game. She broke her leg while tripping on a curb and died when a blood clot shot to her heart. And mine.

We used to talk about having adventures. About saving our money and running away together to the South of France. We wanted to go topless and have French men admire us. We wanted them to look at us with a smoldering, European desire, and say things that we couldn't understand. She died before I found out that the beach on the boardwalk in Nice is rocky and uncomfortable, and that French men think they're too good for American girls, unless they're girls with a lot of money.

Natalie would have liked Dewalt's advice to me. I think she would have even liked Dewalt. One night he plopped down on the stool beside me. I usually sit on the third stool from the corner, and feel put upon if strangers perch their butts on my spot. Dewalt said he drives a Zamboni. At first I thought it was a sports car until he said it was the machine that smoothes out the ice during hockey games.

His chest puffed up as he bragged about his hockey friends like they were movie stars or millionaires. The Big Dogs, he called them. Dewalt wasn't bad looking at all, with tousled blonde hair and playful eyes. His hands were small. I imagined it would take larger hands to drive one of those ice machines. Big hands wrapped in insulated gloves.

When he spoke, I watched his chunky mustache bounce – and I wondered how the Zamboni cleared away the blood from the ice. His lip curled when I asked about the blood. "Red Ice," was all he said.

He rolled up the sleeves on his flannel shirt and showed me jagged scars that he'd gotten from breaking up fights on the ice. A small tattoo on the up-side of his right forearm looked homemade. The thin, uneven letters spelled, Dr. Smooth. My eyes traveled down to his small hands. Then, as if he'd known me forever, Dewalt offered to get me free tickets to come to a game, and see him work.

Despite myself, I started telling him about Louie leaving me. About how Louie wanted a son real bad and no matter how much we tried, he called me lazy for not giving him one. Every night when we'd go to bed, I'd get a talking-to that felt like a scolding. The more he talked, the colder the fire inside me got, until it was nothing more than lifeless ashes. I'd close my eyes and want to turn my back to him. But I stayed until he was the one who left.

Dewalt got a knot between his eyebrows and listened like he knew how I felt. Then he moved his hand to my shoulder. It felt bigger than it looked. He said it was time for me to decide whether I was going to live my life as a stick or as a puck.

I was sounding like a bleeding-heart and changed the subject from Louie to Natalie. I told Dewalt about the time we found a diary in a second hand store that smelled like tomcats and old doilies full of dust and starch. It was a leather bound book with a locking clasp and gold, fancy writing on the cover that said "A Line A Day." A girl named Doris Hartman had written in it fifty years before we found it. We stretched out on the linoleum floor and read every page, like Peeping Toms gawking through an old windowpane. The ink on the pages looked like thin, blue thread set free from its spool.

Doris was a rich girl and her dainty handwriting told of dancing parties and long ago luxury liner trips.

February 8 – Saturday – Arrived in Hong Kong. Shopped on shore – Had dinner with Billie Pape and Mr. Nelson joined us after dinner for dancing – a peach of a time – had 4 "cut-in's" – could only dance two. One was with Mr. Bates, much to Pape's distress. Oh! How I love to dance.

March 30 – Monday – The peak of so much change of climate came today. I fainted, falling head first down the stone stairs of the Imperial Hotel. Mr. Bolton carried me to my room, and dressed my wounds. It made me terribly nervous and I couldn't go to the Smiths' for lunch. I'm lonesome and disgusted with Tokyo. I miss Jamie and regret I must start school in San Andreas before my folks arrive.

For me, reading the diary entries was like crawling through an escape hatch. I wasn't sure if Natalie felt the same way, and I guess I didn't really care, because I bought the diary for her as a birthday present. We decided it would be great fun to search for the girl who wrote in the book. Maybe, just maybe, she would still be alive. Louie didn't want us to go, but when Natalie and I got something in our minds, we were power.

Dewalt liked hearing about me and Natalie, and bought me a beer. We touched mugs and he said, "Here's to Natalie. Ya miss her, don't ya?" I told him life since she died is like breathing only halfway in.

Natalie had the beauty of a proud animal. She had strong bones covered with tight, umber-shaded skin. She saw things through troubled puppy eyes, the color of tobacco, and said things through heavy lips. When we met, on the handball court in third grade, I wanted to touch her skin that shined liked a waxed dining table, and hold her hand that had big knuckles.

Our friendship was instant. It was comfortable, like high top sneakers that are tied real loose. We were iron particles drawn into the same magnetic field, Natalie and I. She had a wonderful name. Natalie Dorotea Ontario Salamanca Martinez. I memorized it and liked to say it out loud. Both our last names started with M, Martinez and Mitchell, and we called ourselves the m&m's even after we both got married. Natalie twice, Garcia and Rivera. Me once, Louie Chapman.

My tongue was feeling loose but Dewalt didn't seem to mind, so I talked about Louie some more. About how we met. About his yellow hair, thick like lamb's wool. He had a sweet, flat face, like a koala bear's, with bulging eyes, and he talked nonstop. Louie sometimes sought support from the "Low-Frequency Noise Sufferers Association," an organization that helps people who hear a hum inside their heads but don't suffer from a hearing disorder.

We met at the Noisy Pelican on his first day in town. He stopped by after emptying a truckload of furniture at his new place down the street. Louie leaned towards me when he talked and tapped my arm gently to make a point. That very touch made me light hearted and playful and sexy and alive. He talked a blue streak – and I threw my head back in laughter. I went to his apartment that night to help him set up house – and I'm still there now.

After we got married, it upset him when Natalie and I still called ourselves the m&m's. He said I was a Chapman, and I didn't need to go back to my maiden initial, even for a nickname, but Natalie and I had been friends too long to be called anything else.

When we took the diary and went to find Doris Hartman, we stocked the car with giant bags of candy, both plain and peanut. We drove north, with the windows down, grabbing the wind with our hands. We were headed to Mill's College, near Oakland, where the diary said that Doris went to school.

Before she went off to college, her mother bought her a car that she named "Alexander the Great." Doris called it Alex.

> *August 11 – Monday – Oh! Oh! What a wonderful last few days these have been. Received a letter from dearest Dad – he's sending me a Diamond. I got word from the dressmaker that the formal is ready, and took a ride in Alex today.*

> *August 17 – Monday – Thrills! Thrills! I took my medical exam, completed registration, made out my program and paid the tuition at Mills – all is well.*

216

Natalie seemed more interested in stopping at Gilroy than getting up to Mills. The signs along the road said, GILROY – The Garlic Capital of The World. She said Doris could wait – that I shouldn't make such a big deal.

I was anxious to move on but followed her around as she took her sweet time strolling through the airless tourist shops cluttered with sawdust floors and shelves filled with garlic shaped hats and refrigerator magnets. She flirted with a clerk who recommended garlic as a remedy for headaches, bites, worms, tumors, heart ailments – and God knows what else. Natalie clasped her chin and nodded with interest, like her head was loose. I watched her raven-black hair bounce, the way hair moves in shampoo commercials, when he talked about the magical powers of garlic, and how the Romans took it for strength during battles.

The whole town smelled like a belch. I went back to the car to wait, realizing that Natalie didn't care about Doris the way I did. Natalie made fun of Doris and her spoiled ways – but to me she seemed very lonely. Her parents were never around and I thought of Gloria Vanderbilt, the Poor Little Rich Girl. I got a dull sinking feeling in my heart when reading some of the pages, as if I could feel the long, dark night of her soul. As though she could feel mine, too.

*October 21 – Wednesday – **My 22nd Birthday** – The girls came in my room with a box of "Rocky-Roads" and helped me eat them.*

October 23 – Friday – Oh Dear! I'm sick of being a dumb-bell. Why can't I be like other girls and do things? Can I never overcome my self-consciousness? Is there nothing in me?

Natalie didn't have the kind of ears to hear the pages crying out. She'd grown up in a neighborhood of field workers who had no time for self-pity. Her family lived in a complex of World War II Quonset huts. Fourteen of them stood side by side, looking like giant loaves of steel bread lined up along the train track. For ten years the Martinez family lived in the front half of the third building – until they finally moved into a stucco house far from the trains.

When she read the diary, Natalie could only see the diamonds and cars, and dreamed of the beautiful crystal beads that Doris wore.

November 9 – Tuesday – Mother arrived home today with loads of pretty things. A dress & beautiful fur for me – also several strings of crystal beads.

We wondered what she looked like. Natalie thought of Rita Hayworth or Ann Blythe. I wanted her to look like Ingrid Bergman – the way she looked with Bogart in Casablanca. We talked about meeting her as an old woman.

Dewalt excused himself. I thought he'd gone to the john, but he came back with m&m's from the vending machine by the pay phone. He emptied the bag onto the counter between us and stared at my hair as he dragged each of the red ones over to his side. The rest, he said, were for me. "Red is the color of the strength that pumps through our hearts," he said. "Ya know, your hair reminds me of a halo of strength."

Then, sort of embarrassed, he asked if we ever got to meet Doris, and I told him how we went into the library at Mills College. It was a quiet, empty place, except for the hum of the air-conditioner and the taps of my flip-flops. We asked an overweight woman at the front counter where we could look up an old student. The woman wore a blue nametag that said, Miss Iggy.

"The history annuals are preserved downstairs," she said, with a suspicious stare. We gave her the years Doris was at Mills. "Have a seat at one of the tables. Only staff is allowed in the archives. I'll do my best."

Doris' picture was in three of the books. She looked straight at me with a numb smile. Her skin was as pale as mine but her eyes seemed far away. Her hair was dark, and bobbed with a side-part. In all three photos, she wore crystal beads.

The hairs on my arms rose as footsteps shuffled past. I thought they could be Doris' and didn't look up for fear of disappointment. Time lingered as I looked past the pages into her fixed eyes. Doris had jewels and beautiful clothes, but she didn't have friends, like I had Natalie.

We turned the pages in silence, looking for more. There was no more.

I read the diary out loud another time while Natalie drove home, down the coast. The words were like an echo that bounced back at me.

December 27 – Friday – Feelin kinda heavy and blue. What a year it has been. We never know from one minute to the next where we'll be.

We talked about our next trip – to San Andreas where Doris lived. Back then, we were on a journey to the past, but now I can't go back for the young girl who wrote to us so long ago, not without Natalie. Hell, I can't even get off the barstool.

I stopped talking and looked over to see that the red m&m's were gone. Dewalt's face was serious. "Natalie might not have known what you felt, but I do."

I smiled for the first time in a year, and I told Dewalt that I'd like to see him drive the Zamboni at the next hockey game.

— NANCY KLANN

219

It's never too late – in fiction or in life – to revise.

– Nancy Thayer

Trespass

She stood at the edge of the porch on loose floorboards, pressing an index finger against her brow to shield her eyes from the burn of a white hot sky. A column of dust rose on the horizon, dust or smoke or something like it, out of place here. She squinted against the merciless glare. "Harmon," she called, "there's someone approachin'."

"Can't be," he hollered back. "Ain't been no one on this property for years." He tilted his head back, catching the last drops of tequila from an empty bottle. Swaggering into the light of midday, he joined her on the splintered floorboards and damn if she wasn't right. A truck approached, kicking up dust along the narrow rut that doubled for road.

"God forsaken trespassers," he spat. "Who do they think they are coming onto my land?"

Close to the border, she and Harmon scraped out a living in the unforgiving desert, raising cattle on the parched earth. The closest supply town, Ragweed, lay twenty miles west. But Ray Anne rarely showed face.

She tugged her faded work shirt over narrow hips, smoothing back thin wisps of graying hair. "Maybe there's trouble?" she wondered aloud. Truth was, most folks didn't wander onto their land. Most folks knew better not to.

"Hell with that," he slurred in his stupor. "Let 'em all die. What do I care?" He wheeled the hulk of his frame back into darkness, that spare house with the curtains all drawn, light spilling through random cracks in the walls. She followed him in like a shadow and watched him curl into a heap on the mattress. Sure enough his jaw grew slack, and in no time at all his ragged breath grated the silence.

Relieved, she tiptoed back to the porch, then shielding her eyes she caught sight of the truck in the undulating heat. The load in the back came into focus: a truck full of people, not livestock as she'd first believed. She surveyed the scene, thought they'd taken a wrong turn. No one in their right mind would wander onto this ranch, unless they expected the worst.

Ray Anne considered saddling Dyno, the roan horse, so she could ride out to investigate. She stepped off the porch, anxiously glancing back every few steps making sure not to disturb Harmon. Mean old son of a bitch. He hated people. Hell, he even hated *her*. Tolerated in Ragweed, he'd drive cattle in, conduct his business, drink his fair share, then return, demanding a meal before passing out for the night. No sign of him, he'd most likely snore his way long until supper.

Why the heck not? She strolled out to the barn in defiance, saddled the horse and bolted in a cloud of dust.

At a comfortable distance, she halted, squinting at the dark outline of a man. He stood in the shadow of the truck waving his hat. "Hello?" he shouted in a questioning voice. She rode up beside him, climbed down off the horse.

"What you all doin'?" she asked. "You know this is Harmon's ranch, right? Signs posted everywhere. No Trespassing. Harmon means business. He'll shoot."

The man replaced the hat on his bare head. "We're lookin' for Ribald. R-I-B . . .," he began to spell out the name of the ranch ten miles east.

"No need to spell it. I know who they are. Ten miles that way," she pointed. "You don't want to end up here," she warned. "Best hightail it now, before you find yourselves toast."

She surveyed the truck. Silently looking her over, the men studied her rail thin frame. "Get on out of here," she repeated. "If John Ribald's expectin' you, you'd best move on."

The first shot rang out like a clap of thunder. The unmistakable sound of a bullet whizzed past. In confusion, the men scurried out of the truck. Leather soles sounded on hardscrabble earth, shuffling in naked silence. Ray Anne stood her ground. Crazy bastard, she thought.

Someone shouted, "God damn it, take cover!" But there was no place to hide. Desert cactus offers no refuge. A second gunshot tore through the air, the bullet ricocheting off the front bumper. It rang like a bell. Panicked, the men huddled behind the truck, a few desperately diving beneath it.

"You miserable son of a bitch!" Ray Anne screamed. The third bullet caught her below the rib cage. She stumbled in shock, legs buckling beneath her. Serrated rocks scraped her shoulder blades, tore at the flesh on her legs. Fiery sun penetrated her gaze as she lay in a pool of blood. As the blood cooled, it soothed her. Welcome contrast to the burning hot wound in her abdomen. She lay there alone as the bullets whizzed past, flies relentlessly buzzing like an odd lullabye.

An eerie silence permeated the space around them. High in the thermals, buzzards wheeled and tipped their wings. "Let's get the hell out of here!" one of the men shouted. In a panic, they piled into the truck. One or two glanced at Ray Anne, but most looked away. Dust rose in a whirlwind as the truck bumped along in retreat.

Harmon ducked into the sun-pierced darkness beneath the tumbledown roof. "Damn those vagrants, that'll show them. Who the hell do they think they are, trespassing onto my land?" Unrequited silence met the blast of his words. "Ray Anne, where are you Woman? I don't smell no dinner!" He tossed his sweat soaked hat on the wooden chair by the door. Damn if his back didn't ache. Inch by inch he unraveled muscle and bone atop the mattress, succumbing to an interminable stupor. As the stars popped out, he snored.

Snored as her eyes glazed over, and her spirit soared skyward.

— ELAINE PIKE

223

*In any real good subject, one
has only to probe deep enough
to come to tears.*"

– Edith Wharton

A Trip to Idaho

On a mild Saturday afternoon in September, I am seated on an uncomfortable metal chair at the back of a small auditorium, watching the guests arrive for a memorial service. Rows of the same brown/gray metal chairs face a podium placed in front of the closed curtains of a stage. Couples, mostly young, some with children, drift in, greet the family of the deceased, and fall into conversation. The family members, the Johnsons, dressed in black, gray, white, stand about in clumps, talking. I do my job, which is to observe, and to take note, to pay attention as the participants gather to honor the dead man. He and all these people, perhaps fifty, are strangers to me, except for one.

My friend Pam and I have driven across two states to attend the memorial service for her nephew, Robert, a young man in his 30's who killed himself.

As we drove, Pam told me the story of Robert's last months: divorce, financial problems, conflict over his child's visitation schedule. But others suffer those agonies and endure. Others escape the beckoning abyss. Robert did not. His response to life's calamities was to embrace the abyss, triggering one of our deepest fears — a loved one choosing self-annihilation instead of reaching out for help. Because we would all be eager to aid, to comfort, to do anything to save the lost — wouldn't we?

The mourners gradually seat themselves. The crowd hushes as a tall, sandy-haired man dressed in a flannel shirt and khaki slacks steps behind the podium and begins to speak. He introduces himself as the local minister who has been asked by the family to preside over the service. His manner is gentle, low-key, but his words cut. He speaks of the anguish of suicide for friends and family, the guilt and failure we feel, for we had all failed the dead man, Robert, and missed his unspoken cries for help.

The minister recites lines of the Psalmist feeling forsaken, despairing as the overwhelming darkness engulfs him. But somehow, in that word, the minister finds a tiny hint of hope that at the last minute Robert found comfort, found God.

Ah, the consolation of religion.

One by one, family members come to the podium to speak of the dead man.

His brother describes Robert as the pace-setter of the family, setting the bar for his siblings, cheering them on to reach it. His sister weeps as she tells of Robert's love of nature. His father has no tears, but his words are awash with sorrow and loss, then brighten with a tale of Robert's love of humor.

Robert's mother, Lana, tastefully dressed in her tailored brown jacket and slacks, tells of her joy when she first saw her son at two days old, given up by his birth mother, an 18-year-old woman who knew she could not raise a child alone. Lana, too, is calm. Perhaps three months of tears have given her the fortitude to speak today.

Then Amy comes to the podium. Taller than the Johnsons, her pale face framed with blond hair, she has the poise and bearing of a regal visitor. Emitting great dignity and warmth, she tells the story of a young woman who had spent a few nights with a soldier, then had to tell him of his unborn child. The man was not interested in fatherhood, and she wanted more for her child than she, a teenager, could give him. So two days after giving birth, she signed the papers and her son went to the Johnsons, a mother and father who had been longing for a child, and had the means to secure his future. Amy goes on to describe how, just a few years ago, Robert found her. She knew when she saw the return address of the adoption agency on the envelope that it was he asking to contact her. And she welcomed the contact, the close relationship they were in the process of forming.

An amazing woman, I think. Strong, secure, to tell her story to strangers.

Then, over the speakers, a song floats through the room, a song that Robert loved, celebrating sky and clouds, hills and wind — the beauty of our world.

Music reaches where words fall short; I weep as I have not allowed myself to for many years. I weep for Robert, a man I did not know, for my daughter, for my mother, for all my dead. I weep for myself, deprived of their luminous love. I weep for all of us who have to die and for those left to weep.

I am not alone in my tears. Pam and I hug, and when I open my eyes I see many others tear-stained and embracing.

Lana announces that the ashes will now be taken to Robert's favorite fishing spot beside the river, and there he will be sent on his final journey.

Pam and I get in her car and join the others bound for the river, two miles away. We park on the overpass and follow groups of two and three down the path to the clearing next to the water. We are surrounded by a late-afternoon panorama of lush grassland ending in the gray peaks of the Tetons, the sky cluttered with billowy clouds, a light wind caressing us.

Robert's sister appears carrying a yellow tote — the ashes, Pam tells me. The minister arrives.

I leave the group by the water and climb back to the overpass, looking down at the riverside scene. Being a participant is too painful. I return to my role as observer, as witness. The minister reads from the Bible but I cannot hear his words. He closes the book and heads bow in prayer.

The sister takes a box from the tote, an ordinary looking box, and places it on the earth at the water's edge. Two women now preside: the mother and the birth mother.

Lana, the mother, opens the box, takes a handful of white powder and flings it into the air. It settles on the water and drifts away. Amy, the birth-mother, takes a handful of ashes and drops it into the water. Both women throw ashes into the river. Then Amy removes her shoes and steps into the water. She stands in the river and offers ashes to the current. With her grace, her deliberate, unhurried movements she is a goddess, one of the Fates, enacting an ancient ritual.

We watch, bearing witness to this ultimate pain and redemption.

The slow strong water takes the freight given it and carries it away.

— CAROL SANDERS

227

Failure: is it limitation? Bad timing? It's a lot of things. It's something you can't be afraid of, because you'll stop growing. The next step beyond failure could be your biggest success in life.

— Debbie Allen

Lunar Colonies

This city is named
for Caesar Augustus.
Can't you hear it?
Zaragoza.

I still get myself
lost here, even as I've
learned the curves
of the *Casco Viejo,*

the spiral of
the city center around
the *Plaza de España*, the
banks of the *Rio Ebro.*

I live on the far side
of the river, next to the
Carrefour, a big store
like a J.C. Penney's

with a supermarket in the
basement, I live with a host
family: a host Mom, a host
sister, a host Dad. I'm 15.

At night I call home to
my real Mom in New Jersey.
I call her from the future, in
España we're 6 hours ahead.

They found a Roman city here
buried beneath the streets, concrete
poured over the past, concrete
poured over ash and bone.

On my first night in Zaragoza,
I got lost in the dark by
the *Carrefour*, cobblestone
streets. I stopped a couple

to ask them for directions, I
don't even know
what it was that
came out of my mouth.

They waved their hands
in the air, gracefully,
like dancers:
Sign language.

I can't pantomime over
the phone, how can I explain
to her? Everything's different
here. Even me.

Here I am, floating up
in the air like their hands,
I never have the
right words here.

The moon's a brass ring
in the sky. When
I look up, I see
what I've become:

I'm a spacewoman,
heading for a crash.
They've built a city on
the dark side of the moon.

They've built it up
around the ruins
of an ancient spaceship.
They've named the city for me.

— MOIRA WILLIAMS

Poetry is life distilled.

— Gwendolyn Brooks

Three Wishes

"Watch where you're putting that size twelve foot of yours," squealed a tiny voice from somewhere inside my shower stall. With heart beating at the rate of some abnormal count, I searched within and without my watery cubicle to see who or what dared to enter my steamy domain.

A black and white striped critter, no longer than an over-sized paperclip, glared at me while struggling, without success, to escape. I was standing on its hairless tail, the length of half a Q-tip.

"Let me go you big lummox. Go stand on someone your own size, maybe a dinosaur or an NFL behemoth," it demanded, spitting soapsuds at me with every word.

"What in God's name are you and where did you come from and why?" I sputtered, silently questioning my sanity.

My uninvited shower-mate, who introduced itself as *Virgil*, quickly explained that it was a mezepo, a breed of prehistoric miniature meerkat, zebra and possum. Its beady eyes, striped coat and tail verified its pedigree. Virgil informed me that in my hurry to test a recently purchased industrial-size electric plunger I somehow managed to suction it up through my plumbing system as an uninvited guest.

"Send me home as soon as possible," Virgil demanded, "and to show my appreciation, I'll grant you three wishes."

"Three wishes! Ha! You're no genie and I'm too old for fairy tales."

The mezepo sighed. "I guarantee I do have three wishes in escrow for you and if you'll satisfy my request, I'll keep my word and make your wishes come true. But you must remember to think before you make each wish because you will get exactly what you ask for."

The shower's warm temperature finally restored feeling and mobility to my numb limbs, but obviously affected that part of my brain considering a proposition from a figment of my imagination. Oh what the hell, I thought,

I'll go along with this and maybe I can ignore how my dietary indulgences have increased my waistline since yesterday.

However, before releasing my prisoner, I needed more time to mull over its offer. In view of the fact that life provides me with many material blessings, I wondered what I could possibly wish for that I didn't already possess. Well, I thought, I don't have a pet. Perhaps my figment might be a loving companion to come home to each day. It's a cute little thing in a bizarre sort of way. Maybe, in time, I could actually grow quite fond of it.

"While you're thinking up there, I'm drowning down here," my potential pet sputtered. "Could you give me some cover with your manly endowments until you come to a decision – preferably sooner than later."

Without removing my foot, I attempted to accommodate the little thing even as I debated the pros and cons of his sales pitch. Suddenly I caught a glimpse of my reflection in the mirror opposite the shower. Like the wham of a thunderbolt I realized the physique of my twenties could be restored with one of the wishes. Then I could once again relish the youthful pleasures that have made me today's dissipated wreck.

"Okay, you have a deal, but before setting you free I feel I should hang you by your tail on the towel hook until you've fulfilled your promises."

"Are you always this suspicious?" Virgil groaned with disgust.

"Just cautious. So in exchange for your release, Virgil, my first wish is to be twenty-two once more. My second wish is for an eighteen-year-old virgin to revive the excitements of my past."

Within seconds I became a sculpted Adonis with a gorgeous raven-haired Aphrodite beckoning me to her side.

"Wow! I'm magnificent," I marveled as my goddess caressed me. "Wish my ex-wives could see me now!"

In the blink of an eye my bathroom was filled with five withered old crones screeching like a pack of banshees.

– Joy Blank

234

Walking in the City, Part 1

The crisp cool air whips across your face, making your hair jump around. Colors are vivid blue, greens and reds. How delightful the sound the cable car makes as the throngs of happy tourists wave from their perches alongside the car. They laugh with excitement as the operator warns them of a curve up ahead. You wave back at a little girl gripping the handrail and squealing. Your smile meets her smile.

Chinatown stretches out before you, a mélange of odor...garlic and fish; an old Chinese man teeters on the sidewalk, and you are ready to catch him. The decaying, mysterious oriental style buildings seem like secret dens where fortunes have been made or lost. You stop and gape at a building you walk by nearly everyday, but now it stands out like you are seeing it for the first time. With a slow intake of breath you tell your beloved how fascinating the building is, and he nods. You buy trinkets at one of the Chinese Bazaars, earrings that cost $2, green tea and a cheap wooden backscratcher for a buck. Beloved looks at you with doe eyes and says he will scratch your back for you any time, backscratcher or not. There is warmness that emanates from your heart and reaches all the way to your toes.

The colorful and endearing characters in North Beach make you giggle out loud as they try to entice you into their strip clubs. Attractive Italians beckon you to their restaurants that reek of garlic and freshly baked bread. Beloved grabs your hand and pulls you towards a menu. He wants the pesto; you want the ravioli. You both like the same foods; you agree on just about everything. You will eat there later, splitting a bottle of wine and eating bread with olive oil until you burst. You will take the bottle home and make a candle out of it to remember the evening by.

You walk the narrow streets up to Coit Tower where you look down on the City as the sun sets and lights start to twinkle in windows. You can see all the way to the wine country and all the way to Mt. Diablo in the east. A big freighter from Korea moves surprisingly swiftly into the Bay under the Golden Gate. Someone asks you directions and you laugh as you try to tell them how to get to Lombard Street without getting lost. A homeless man calls you sweetheart and asks for some change; you can't help but smile at him. The beloved gives him a handful of change and the man smiles back and says *God bless you*. You feel blessed as if that man might be God himself. Your eyes are wide open as the night comes on, you smell jasmine and salt from the ocean, the skyline is lit up. You are lit up. You are happy.

Walking back home you stop for a sundae at Ghirardelli's and a baby bestows you with a charming ice cream smeared smile. Darling, you think. You can see your reflection in the parlor mirrors as you smile at the baby, your teeth white, your hair tousled, and you look so good you could be a fashion model.

You and Beloved walk off your dinners and dessert by taking the steps up to Russian Hill. He holds your hand and you both decide to run up the steps. He breaks away, but lets you catch up. Up ahead he leans over a step staring down at something. As you approach, you see an enormous, grotesque potato bug on the stairs, you both shriek and run and then run back to examine the prehistoric looking creature again. It moves and you both run again and collapse into laughter when you reach the top. He holds you close as you take one more look back at the breathtaking view.

Walking in the City, Part 2

The sun is out, but the air is cold and the hair you so carefully brushed is quickly whipped into a mass of snarls. You have to wait for the cable car packed with obese tourists with idiotic grins to cross the intersection, you try not to look at them, and their smiles only make you feel sad.

Chinatown stinks like garbage, old rotting fish parts, and some kind of sewer smell; you hold your breath. An ancient Chinese man hawks and spits a golf-ball-sized wad of phlegm in front of you on the sidewalk, nearly hitting your face. You want to gag. The cheap junk from the shops spills out on the sidewalks and you are forced to walk in the street to get passed the sheep-like tourists being corralled from one rip off to the next.

In North Beach the filthy smut shops gape at you like open orifices begging you to come fill them. Plastic dildos and obnoxious hucksters make you look away, your face burning. A bum demands your change and a smile, you sneer, he says fuck you, yuppie bitch. Your blood pressure skyrockets and you bite your tongue. Italians with phony accents wave menus in front of you as you make your way up Columbus. They call you Ma'am and give fake sickly sweet smiles. You look down with a scowl.

You see your reflection in a window - stoop shouldered, lined face, dark circles under eyes, a poster child for heartbreak. A snot-nosed crying baby screams in defiance as its mother tries to cram it into the stroller. Annoyance makes you cringe.

You walk to Coit Tower and the wind chills you inside out. The City is barely visible through a gray fog. A tourist approaches as if to ask for directions, but she doesn't, instead she turns away from you and asks a couple standing near the wall. Its getting dark, you jam your hands in your pockets and head toward Russian Hill. You pass the festive lights of Ghirardelli's and ignore the loud tourists lined up to feed their faces with the sweet goo. You take the stairs up the hill, your muscles aching with every step. Darkness has fallen and the lights from the foggy bay are barely visible. The cement stairs seem relentless as you march up, your hair wet with the mist. At the top of the stairs, you look back down; hopefully, trying to spot a potato bug... but there is nothing, just the steps going back down into the darkness.

— Tracy Knox

Real literature, like travel, is always a surprise.

— Alison Lurie

Redlands

The day was hot when we went back.

The dirt there is RED, and it used to be covered in Orange Groves.

Used to be ...

Awash with the sweetness of tiny blossoms. White. Thousands upon thousands of rolling groves spraying into the air, a citrus bloom. Imagine the Night. A cricket chirping alone. The moon. Nectar. Youth.

I'm talking now about my mother's college.

The day was hot when we went back. Fifty years later.

There are pathways back.

Freeways. Metallic roaring hulks grinding gears flash in the sun. California. Redlands.

I'm keeping it together.

The map is on my lap.

But I'm not looking at it.

It's always the blossoms that distract me. The blossoms throbbing in air. Beating music on the windows. Hugging my temples until they give in.

My mother is beautiful. Still as beautiful as a delicious blossom, slightly crinkled these fifty years later. Driving. We are going to the reunion "luncheon." My mother smiles at me. Her eyes are pebbles of green jade found in a mountain stream. Mine are fool's gold, slightly dirty. We connect. Blossom to blossom.

She has packed my lunch in a paper sack with food I will eat near the university library.

The lunch is white turkey on Ezekiel bread, three boiled eggs, an apple, orange, banana bread with frosting that sticks to the Saran Wrap.

There is something sacred about this, this so-called "lunch."

A paper sack to drip tears on.

Because I am 46, and my mother is 70.

It's been a long time.

Hot outside. 105. Like hair dryers held to our faces.

I feel the heat as I glance down at my veined hand where a piece of paper trembles.

Ah yes.

The map.

From the frantic snaky labyrinth of freeways, we glide suddenly into the stately time warp that is Redlands. Looming above us along the shaded drives are the Castles of Reason: "Literature" "History" "Science" – a library that looks like the Parthenon.

There!

The tennis courts. Shrouded in bush lushness behind a chain link fence. I see my father fifty years ago jaunty on the clay courts. His winning yelps pure music. His sweat fragrant. Sweet. Salty. Under his arms soft tender hairs.

Look at those steps!

The pixie princess with pom-poms. Who is it? My mother. Saddle-shoes and all.

Her brunette coif bounces like a shampoo commercial. Her skin is vanilla ice cream. And the smile. The smile. A glimmering thing. What is it? Butterfly dust?

Bobbing in the clear liquor of her nectar-ovaries, I float.

Round.

Flawless.

An egg.

I open the sack lunch in the library. The white boiled eggs are cool.

The sandwich seems to sweat.

I have the 1955 yearbook in the quiet carrel.

The black and white picture of my mother is there. She thrusts her bouncy pom-pom skyward where it plumes and fountains. She has trotted up the stone steps in her song-leader outfit and turned to smile for the picture. The wind has blown her hair up in a celebratory flare. The sun gleams on her cheeks, her teeth. Her vibrant youth jumps off the page and smacks me in the face.

God Damn.

I rub the egg on my cheek.

It's skin cool stone. Smooth.

When I find my father's picture, the picture I have never seen in the section marked "Seniors" the little blond hairs on my arms stand on end.

I see all the men I have ever loved in his young face. Many men.

I could put my hands into his dark hair and be home. I stare at him. I search his eyes.

I don't eat the egg.

I eat the banana bread, licking the frosting from the Saran Wrap.

I peek from my carrel to see the clock. It's suddenly two minutes to 1:00. I will meet my mother at the Chapel at 1:00 as agreed when we separated.

As I exit the library the heat of the day blasts me. But it is a dry sizzling heat with piney sap in it.

Young people pass me like flowing waters, streams, trailing scents, words, glints, bits of Magpie chatter. Quick, almost skipping. Hurrying on their way to somewhere.

I walk.

Deeper into the damp cool heart of campus, vast expanse of immaculate lawns, damp mowed grass sugary in the air, massive oaky creaking limbs, dapple shadow show. On the far side, concealed by the knarled arms, the oaks overgrown, are the girls' dorms. And there I know what I see.

Her Window.

Window window window. I see curtains blowing back. I see yearning GIRLface. Her exhalation of hopes, her giggling romances, and telephone talk. Pencils sharpened. The clack of her typewriter. Her bright footsteps in the hall. How she yawns turning from her book, twirling a lock of hair, absently gazing green eyes. Curling her hair. Painting her nails. Talking on the phone, spinning to laugh. I see her flush the toilet, pull up her panties. I see her slide the red stick of lipstick carefully over the arch of her lips. Thinking about some boy. Her bright and eager wave.

Hi!

Lipstick on her teeth.

Oh blossom! Oh beautiful! Oh my heart's darling! Ever ever ever how will I find you again, my Girl with the nectar-nest of eggs and pom-poms and smile, oh, ever smile. When will you climb out your window again when the moon is painted real, and the blossoms are exploding so slowly?

I was there.

Run your lithe legs. Back to me. Return. My flower. My blossom. My tender darling. My mother, sister, Girl. Not to be bruised and crushed. Not to wilt in this cruel heat.

Be splashed with water. Inhale.

SHE has returned.

I see my mother standing at the front of the Chapel waiting for me at 1:00 p.m.

She has dark glasses on. I can't see her eyes.

She smiles. She takes a step toward me. She sees me.

And suddenly quickened, the remains of my sack lunch still in hand, I stride over the grass, beneath the undulating boughs of the oaken witnesses, almost like one of the Young.

— SHERRILL ERICKSON

*Writing is harder than anything else; at least
starting to write is. It's much easier to wash dishes.
When I'm writing I set myself a daily quota of
pages, but nine times out of ten I'm doing those
pages at four o'clock in the afternoon because I've
done everything else first...But once I get flowing
with it, I wonder what took me so long.*

— Kristin Hunter

Meeting of the Minds at the Salon

Without a shred of guilt, Anne confesses she often finds
an unexpected and unexplained peace during her husband's absence.

I don't need a man to rectify myself, Shirley confides. The most profound
relationship I'll ever have is the one with myself.

Mahalia says it's easy to be independent when a woman's got money.

Yes, money and a room of her own, Virginia adds.

And Sophia says mistakes are part of the dues paid for a full life.

Martha thinks happiness or misery depends on disposition, not circumstance.

Anais says: We don't see things as they are; we see them as we are.

Janis says: Don't compromise yourself. You're all you've got.

Find out what you're good at, and then do that, says Katherine.

Sister Mary advises: To be successful, the first thing to do is fall in love
with your work.

Any woman who writes is a survivor, Tillie announces.

I really only ask for time to write it all - time to write my books.
Then I don't mind dying. I live to write, the other Katherine says.

Gertrude scoffs: Everybody's life is full of stories. Your life
is full of stories. My life is full of stories. All very occupying.
Not really interesting. What's interesting is how the stories are told.

Joyce says great works deal with the human soul caught in the stampede
of time unable to gauge the profundity of what passes over it.

It's all in the art. You get no credit for living, V.S. says.

Vivian concludes: So what actually happens is only raw material.
All that matters is what we make of it.

And that's enough, Eudora says.

– MaryAnn Easley with thanks to:

Anne Shaw, Shirley MacLaine, Mahalia Jackson, Virginia Woolf, Sophia Loren, Martha
Washington, Janis Joplin, Katherine Anne Porter, Sister Mary Lauretta, Tillie Olsen, Katherine
Mansfield, Gertrude Stein, Joyce Carol Oates, V.S. Pritchett, Vivian Gornick, Eudora Welty

I really believe people are called to a literary life like others are called to a theological life or a religious life but publishing is a business that is really hard. Hard on your heart. Hard on your soul. Hard on your everything.

— Anne Lamott

ANTHOLOGY CONTRIBUTORS

ENCORE

Windflower Press
www.windflowerpress.com

Mission Statement

Windflower Press is the writer's best friend. Offering classes, critique, peer coaching, workshops, editing, publishing, and book launches, we take care of the details so that writers can do what they are meant to do – write.

The *"She Writes"* Anthology features poetry, short fiction, essays, and memoir excerpts by women and offers a way for established authors to showcase their work and mentor aspiring writers as they build a platform.

At Windflower Press, we understand writers because we are writers, too.

Write what should not be forgotten.
> – Isabel Allende